THE ULTIMATE CARIBBEAN COOKBOOK

TRADITIONAL CARIBBEAN COOKING MADE EASY, QUICK AND DELICIOUS WITH AUTHENTIC CARIBBEAN RECIPES

Elena J. Bearden

TABLE OF CONTENT

1. AUTHENTIC PUERTO RICAN SOFRITO RECIPE 6
2. BEST PERNIL EVER 7
3. BACALAO A LA VIZCAINA (BASQUE-STYLE CODFISH STEW) 8
4. ISLAND BITES: BUDÍN PUERTORRIQUEÑO 10
5. GRILLED SKIRT STEAK WITH RED PEPPERS & ONIONS 11
6. COQUITO PUERTORRIQUEÑO 12
7. SURULLITOS DE MAIZ (CORNMEAL STICKS) 13
8. COMO HACER COQUITO PUERTORRIQUEÑO 14
9. SORULLITOS DE MAIZ 15
10. DADDY EDDIE'S ROAST PORK (PERNIL), PUERTO RICAN-STYLE 16
11. COQUITO RECIPE 18
13. EASY PINA COLADA FRENCH TOAST 20
14. EGGNOG BREAD PUDDING WITH COQUITO SAUCE 21
15. GANDULE RICE 22
16. ADOBO SEASONING 24
17. HORCHATA DE ARROZ (MEXICAN RICE DRINK) 25
18. TRY THESE BELOVED PUERTO RICAN RECIPES 26
19. JOY'S GREEN BANANA SALAD 29
20. MAICENA (CORN PUDDING) 30
21. MANGO PUDDING (FLAN DE MANGO) 31
22. PUERTO RICAN MOFONGO 32
23. EASY CHICKEN MOFONGO RECIPE 33
24. MY CLASSIC PUERTO RICAN CARNE GUISADA 36
25. PASTELES WITH YUCA AND PLANTAINS 37
26. PASTELÓN (SWEET PLANTAIN LASAGNA) 39
27. PUERTO RICAN STUFFED PEPPERS 40
28. PIÑA COLADA SORBET 42
29. PIQUE - PUERTO RICAN HOT SAUCE - RECIPE 43
30. POLLO (CHICKEN) FRICASSEE FROM PUERTO RICO 44
31. POLVARONES 45

32. PONCHE DE RON DE PUERTO RICO (COQUITO) 46
33. NATILLA (PUERTO RICAN CUSTARD DESSERT) 47
34. PUERTO RICAN CABBAGE, AVOCADO, AND CARROT SALAD 48
35. COQUITO | PUERTO RICAN COCONUT NOG 49
36. PUERTO RICAN EMPANADAS 50
37. PUERTO RICAN ROAST PORK SHOULDER (PERNIL) 53
38. PUERTO RICAN SANCOCHO 55
39. PUERTO RICAN–STYLE SHEPHERD'S PIE 57
40. PUERTO RICAN STEAMED RICE 58
41. RISOTTO WITH PIGEON PEAS AND PULLED PORK (RISOTTO CON GANDULES Y PERNIL) 59
42. SLOW COOKED PUERTO RICAN PORK (PERNIL) 60
43. SLOW COOKER PUERTO RICAN SHREDDED PORK 61
44. PUERTO RICAN SOFRITO FROM SCRATCH RECIPE 63
45. STUFFED TURKEY LEGS 64
46. SWEET PLANTAIN PIE RECIPE 65
47. TEA PARTY SANDWICHES (PUERTO RICAN VERSION) 66
48. TEMBLEQUE (PUERTO RICAN COCONUT PUDDING) 67
49. TEMBLEQUE DE COCO (COCONUT TEMBLEQUE) 69
50. TEMBLEQUE (PUERTO RICAN COCONUT PUDDING) 71
51. PUERTO RICAN TOSTONES (FRIED PLANTAINS) 72
52. PUERTO RICAN CHRISTMAS COQUITO 73
53. VEGAN MOFONGO (FRIED MASHED PLANTAINS) 74
54. HOW TO PREPARE THIS RECIPE FOR CHIPOTLE CHICKEN IN THE AIR FRYER 76
55. SHRIMP SOUP (SOPA DE CAMARONES) 77
56. PUPUSAS DE QUESO (EL SALVADORAN CHEESE STUFFED TORTILLAS) 78
57. CHICKEN IN WHITE WINE SAUCE 79
58. EL SALVADORAN ROAST TURKEY 80
59. SALVADORIAN QUEZADILLA 82
60. TAMALES PISQUES 83
61. MOFONGO 85
62. ACCRAS DE MORUE 86
63. AFRICAN ADOBO-RUBBED TUNA STEAKS 88

64. ARROZ CON POLLO PERUANO 90
65. BAKED BANANAS 92
66. MEDITERRANEAN-STYLE WHOLE ROASTED RED SNAPPER 93
67. BANANA SPLIT WITH CURRIED CHOCOLATE-COCONUT SAUCE 95
68. GARLIC MASHED YUCA ROOT 96
69. BUTTERNUT SQUASH WITH WALNUTS AND VANILLA 97
70. CARIBBEAN CHICKEN KEBABS WITH LIME-CAYENNE BUTTER 99
71. CARIBBEAN COCONUT CURRY SAUCE 100
72. CARIBBEAN PUMPKIN AND BLACK BEAN SOUP 101
73. CARIBBEAN RICE AND BLACK BEAN SALAD 102
74. CHICKEN AND PORK STEW WITH PLANTAINS AND POTATOES 103
75. CHILI-RUBBED SALMON WITH AVOCADO SALSA 104
76. CHOCOLATE-ANISE STRAWS 106
77. CHOCOLATE CINNAMON RICE PUDDING 107
78. DAIQUIRI 108
79. CLASSIC HAVANA FRITTATA 109
80. HOW TO MAKE TRINIDAD COCONUT BAKE 110
81. COCONUT FLAN RECIPE 112
82. COCONUT RICE AND PEAS 113
83. COCONUT SHRIMP WITH TAMARIND GINGER SAUCE 115
84. COFFEE-BEAN GRANITA 116
85. CRAB AND CHORIZO FRITTERS 117
86. CRAB AND COCONUT DIP WITH PLANTAIN CHIPS 118
87. CREAM CHEESE FLAN 119
88. CURRY-COCONUT MUSSELS 121
89. DULCE DE PLÁTANO 122
90. DULCE DE PLÁTANO 123
91. GARLIC TOSTONES (FRIED GREEN PLANTAINS) 124
92. SPICED GINGER SIMPLE SYRUP 125
93. GRILLED JAMAICAN JERK PORK CHOPS 126
94. GRILLED FILLET OF BEEF WITH TOMATO GINGER VINAIGRETTE 127
95. GRILLED PINEAPPLE WITH VANILLA MASCARPONE 128

96. GUAVA-STUFFED CHICKEN WITH CARAMELIZED MANGO 129

97. VEGAN HAITIAN SOUP JOUMOU 131

98. PICKLED CABBAGE RECIPE 133

99. HANGER STEAKS WITH 125TH STREET MALANGA MASH 135

100. ISLAND PORK TENDERLOIN (NON-COMPULSORY SALAD) 136

101. JAMAICAN HOT PEPPER SHRIMP 138

102. JAMAICAN JERK CHICKEN 140

103. JAMAICAN JERK POTATO SALAD 141

104. JAMAICAN JERK MARINADE RECIPE 142

105. JERK PORK RECIPE 143

106. KEY LIME CHEESECAKE WITH MANGO RIBBONS 145

107. KEY LIME MASCARPONE "CANNOLI" WITH MANGO SAUCE 147

108. LAMB CHOPS WITH MASHED SWEET POTATOES AND ONIONS 149

109. MANGO LIME SYRUP 151

110. MANGOES FLAMBÉ 151

111. SOFRITO GRILLED BREAD 152

1. AUTHENTIC PUERTO RICAN SOFRITO RECIPE

Prep Time: 15 minutes

Total Time: 15 minutes

Servings: 5 cup of

Ingredients

- 5 green peppers seeded and chop up
- 2 red peppers seeded and chop up
- 4 cubanelle peppers seeded and chop up
- 1 pack or about 12 aji dulce peppers seeded and chop up
- 5 cups of Spanish onions chop up
- 1 cup of garlic chop up
- 1 bunch of recao chop up
- 1 bunch of cilantro chop up

Instructions

1. After everything has been cleaned and the seeds removed, mix them in a food processor or blender in small batches. (They might need to be finished in groups. Onions are excellent for the bottom because, once mixd, they release a lot of liquid.)
2. In a closed container, refrigerate. Anything extra that won't be used within the next two weeks should be refrigerate in tiny containers.

Nutrition

Serving: 0g | Carbs: 0g | Protein: 0g | Fat: 0g | Sat fat: 0g | PolyunSat fat: 0g | MonounSat fat: 0g | Trans Fat: 0g | Cholesterol: 0mg | Sodium: 0mg | Potassium: 0mg | Fiber: 0g | Sugar: 0g | Vit. A: 0IU | Vit. C: 0mg | Calcium: 0mg | Iron: 0mg

2. BEST PERNIL EVER

Prep Time: 15 mins

Cook Time: 5 hrs

Additional Time: 1 day 50 mins

Total Time: 1 day 6 hrs 5 mins

Servings: 12

Ingredients

- 9 cloves garlic
- 1 ½ tbsp olive oil
- 1 ½ tsp salt
- 1 tsp oregano
- ½ tsp ground black pepper
- 1 (7 pound) skin-on, bone-in pork shoulder (picnic) roast
- 1 (1.5 liter) bottle red table wine

Directions

1. Use a mortar and pestle to crush the garlic into tiny pieces. Make a paste by mixing in the oregano, salt, black pepper, and olive oil.
2. Use a sharp knife to slice 12 deep slits spaced a few inches apart in the roast. Incisions on the roast should be filled evenly with seasoned garlic paste.
3. Place the roast in a large basin. Add red wine and fully cover roast. For 24 hours, marinate in the refrigerator with a cover made of plastic wrap.
4. Recycle the red wine. Place the roast in a roasting pan with the fat side facing up and wrap it in foil. Allow to rest for about 30 minutes at room temperature.

5. Set the oven to 400 degrees Fahrenheit (200 degrees C).
6. Place the roast in the preheated oven and lower the temperature to 300°F (150 degrees C). Bake for about 4 hours, or until the middle is just a little pink.
7. up the temperature to 400 degrees Fahrenheit (200 degrees C). Roast should bake for a another hour or more, uncovered, or until the fat is crispy and an instant-read thermometer placed in the center registers 160 degrees F (71 degrees C).
8. After taking it out of the oven, give it 20 to 30 minutes to rest before sliceting.

Cook's Note:

- If you like, you can use 3 tbsp of chop up garlic for the cloves.
- Editor's note: The full amount of red wine is included in the nutritional information for this recipe. There is no set amount of red wine that will be consumed.

3. BACALAO A LA VIZCAINA (BASQUE-STYLE CODFISH STEW)

Prep Time:30 mins

Cook Time:35 mins

Additional Time:8 hrs

Total Time:9 hrs 5 mins

Servings:8

Ingredients

- 1 pound salted cod fish
- 4 medium potatoes, split thick
- 2 medium onions, split
- 4 large hard-boiled eggs, split
- 2 tsp capers

- 2 large cloves garlic, chop up
- ¼ cup of pitted green olives
- 1 (4 ounce) jar roasted red bell peppers, drained
- ½ cup of golden raisins
- 1 large bay leaf
- 1 (8 ounce) can tomato sauce
- ½ cup of extra virgin olive oil
- 1 cup of water
- ¼ cup of white wine

Directions

1. Salted codfish should be soaked for eight hours in about two quarts of water, with three water changes. Codfish is first drained, then it is diced.
2. Potatoes, codfish, onions, hard-boiled eggs, capers, garlic, olives, roasted red peppers, raisins, and 1/2 of every ingredient are placed in a pot in that sequence. After placing the bay leaf on top of the raisins, cover them with half the tomato sauce and half the olive oil. Skip the bay leaf and repeat the layers in the same sequence. Without stirring, add white wine and water to the top.
3. Over medium heat, cover and bring to a boil. Medium-low heat should be used to cook the potatoes for about 30 minutes.

Tips

- This stew is typically served in Puerto Rico with white rice on the side and boiling root vegetables like yucca, yauta, ame, or cooked green bananas. After plating, add a piece of avocado to the side and drizzle extra virgin olive oil over everything. Serving with a side of funche is an additional choice (Puerto Rican polenta).

4. ISLAND BITES: BUDÍN PUERTORRIQUEÑO

Ingredients

- 1 can evaporated milk
- 3 eggs
- 6 slices stale sandwich loaf/split bread
- 1 cup of brown sugar
- 1 tbs vanilla extract
- 1 tsp cinnamon
- 1/4 tsp nutmeg
- raisins
- a pinch of salt

Instructions

1. Mix sugar and eggs in a large bowl. Mix in the salt, vanilla, spices, and milk.
2. With your fingers, crumble the bread, then stir it into the mixture. Stir thoroughly until mixd. The outcome ought to have a few lumps and be a little thicker. Give it five to ten minutes to set.
3. Stir in the raisins to the batter. Move to a baking pan that has been buttered.
4. Bake for 40 to 45 minutes, or until the mixture is set, at 350 degrees Fahrenheit. It is typically served chilled or at room temperature.
5. Budin from Puerto Rico with nmuts Advice
6. You can substitute nuts for the raisins if you don't like them. For a crunchy topping, sprinkle a layer of nuts at the bottom of the pan before adding the batter.
7. You can omit the evaporated milk and add toasted coconut as a garnish.
8. To give the raisins more flavor, soak them in rum.

5. GRILLED SKIRT STEAK WITH RED PEPPERS & ONIONS

Total Time

Prep: 30 min.

marinating Grill: 20 min..

Makes 6 servings

Ingredients

- 1/2 cup of apple juice
- 1/2 cup of red wine vinegar
- 1/4 cup of lightly chop up onion
- 2 tbsp rubbed sage
- 3 tsp ground coriander
- 3 tsp ground mustard
- 3 tsp freshly ground pepper
- 1 tsp salt
- 1 garlic clove, chop up
- 1 cup of olive oil
- 1 beef skirt steak (1-1/2 pounds), slice into 5-in. pieces
- 2 medium red onions, slice into 1/2-inch slices
- 2 medium sweet red peppers, halved
- 12 green onions, trimmed

Directions

1. Mix the first nine ingredients in a small bowl; add the oil gradually while whisking. Put 1-and-a-half cups of marinade in a big basin. Add the beef and stir to coat. Overnight, cover and chill. Keep the remaining marinade covered and chilled.

2. Mix the remaining vegetables and 1/4 cup of the marinade in a big bowl. Red onions and peppers should be covered and grilled for 4-6 minutes on every side, or until they are soft. Grill green onions for 1-2 minutes on every side or until they are soft.
3. Drain beef and throw away marinade. Grill covered over medium heat for 4-6 minutes on every side, or until the meat reveryes the desired degree of doneness (for medium-rare, a thermometer should read 135°; medium, 140°; and medium-well, 145°). During the final 4 minutes of cooking, baste with the remaining marinade. the meat for five minutes.
4. Vegetables should be chop up into bite-sized pieces and placed in a big bowl. Thinly slice the steak against the grain in a diagonal direction; add to the vegetables and blend.

Nutrition Facts

1 serving: 461 calories, 32g fat (7g Sat fat), 67mg cholesterol, 311mg sodium, 12g Carb (5g sugars, 3g fiber), 32g protein.

6. COQUITO PUERTORRIQUEÑO

Prep3 MIN

Total2 HR 8 MIN

Ingredientes

- 1(12 oz.) lata de leche evaporada
- 1(4 oz.) lata de leche condensada azucarada
- 1(4 oz.) lata de crema de coco
- 1cucharadita de canela molida
- 1taza de ron blanco

Instrucciones

1. Remove the evaporated milk, the condensed azucar-flavored milk, the cocoa cream, and the melted canela from the liqueur maker and mix until a uniform liquid is formed.
2. Vaca the ron and stir again.
3. Place the chicken in a glass bottle or jar and place it in the refrigerator for at least two hours.
4. Serve cold with a sprinkle of melted sugar cane on top.

7. SURULLITOS DE MAIZ (CORNMEAL STICKS)

Prep Time:20 mins

Cook Time:15 mins

Total Time:35 mins

Servings:10

Yield:50 sticks

Ingredients

- 2 cups of water
- 1 ¼ tsp salt
- 1 ½ cups of yellow cornmeal
- 5 tbsp white sugar, or as need (Non-compulsory)
- 4 ounces Edam cheese, shredded
- 2 cups of oil for deep frying
- 1 cup of ketchup
- 1 cup of mayonnaise

Directions

1. Bring salt and water to a boil in a saucepan. Add cornmeal and sugar after removing from the fire. Once more, simmer while stirring continually until the mixture begins to come away from the pan's sides. After removing from the heat, thoroughly incorporate Edam cheese.
2. Make balls out of tablespoonfuls of the cornmeal mixture. Then, shape the balls into 3 inch long, thin sticks. To make a dipping sauce, mix mayonnaise and ketchup in a medium bowl. Place aside.
3. In a large, heavy skillet, heat the oil to 375 degrees F. (190 degrees C). Carefully add a few cornmeal sticks to the hot oil, making sure they don't get crowded. Fry for 3 to 4 minutes, or until golden brown. Take out of the hot oil and pat dry with paper towels. Serve with dipping sauce right away.

8. COMO HACER COQUITO PUERTORRIQUEÑO

Ingredientes

- 1 taza de crema de coco (sin azúcar agregada) 250 ml
- 1 lata de leche de coco 400 ml
- 1 lata de leche condensada 305 ml
- 1-2 tazas de ron 250-500ml
- 1 cucharadita de vainilla
- 1 cucharadita de canela en polvo
- ¼ de cucharadita de nuez moscada en polvo opcional
- Un trozo de coco para decorar opcional
- Canela para decorar

Preparación

1. If you intend to relax the coquito, thoroughly launder the bottles and leave them with the mouth below.
2. Place the coconut cream, coconut milk, coconut milk condensed, ron, vanilla, canela, and chop up nuts within the licorice vat. The amount of ron depends on your

preferences; you can add 1 tsp. for a light version or up to 2 tsp. for a stronger version.
3. For a version without alcohol, leave out the ron or replace it with a cucharadita of ron essence.
4. Batte them for a few minutes.
5. Put the crab inside the previously prepared bottles by using an embudo. If you intend to consume it right away, you can serve it in ice-filled containers. To ensure that the flavors are properly concentrated, it is best to keep it chilled for at least 24 hours. It may be necessary to remove it thoroughly before serving after taking it out of the refrigerator.
6. This step is non-compulsory if you want to decorate with trocitos of roasted coconut. Use a vegetable pelter to make cocoa cintas, or use a cheese rallator to directly ralla some cocoa.
7. You can also use coco ralladura to decorate the vases or cups of.
8. Place the cocoa trochitos on top. If desired, you can also sprinkling a little canela or moss-covered nuez.

9. SORULLITOS DE MAIZ

yield: 30 SERVINGS

prep time: 15 MINUTES

cook time: 5 MINUTES

total time: 20 MINUTES

Ingredients

- 2 cups of Water
- 1 tablespoon butter
- 2-4 tbsp granulated sugar
- 1 tsp salt
- 1 1/4 cups of cornmeal
- 1 cup of shredded cheddar cheese

Instructions

1. Water, butter, sugar, and salt should all be mixd in a medium pot over medium heat.
2. Bring to a boil before whisking in the cornmeal gradually. For 3-5 minutes, keep stirring with a spoon until a soft ball forms. After taking the pan off the heat, thoroughly incorporate the cheese.
3. till you can handle it, let cool. Add a small amount of warm water at a time if the dough is crumbly. Add extra cornmeal if dough sticks to your fingers (a little sticky is good). Like playdough, the dough should be bouncy and smooth.
4. Take a tablespoonful of dough and smooth it out between your fingers. Make a log that is three inches long and half an inch wide. Use the leftover dough to repeat.
5. Fry the sorullitos in batches in hot (350°F), at least 1-inch-deep oil. Cook until golden brown, about 3 to 4 minutes. Drain on paper towels after removing from the oil.

Nutrition Information:

YIELD: 30 SERVING SIZE: 1
Amount Per Serving: CALORIES: 43TOTAL FAT: 2gSAT FAT: 1gTRANS FAT: 0gUNSAT FAT: 1gCHOLESTEROL: 5mgSODIUM: 101mgCARBS: 6gFIBER: 0gSUGAR: 2gPROTEIN: 1g

10. DADDY EDDIE'S ROAST PORK (PERNIL), PUERTO RICAN-STYLE

Prep Time:15 mins

Cook Time:4 hrs

Additional Time:9 hrs

Total Time:13 hrs 15 mins

Servings:8

Ingredients

- 10 cloves garlic, or more as need
- ¼ cup of olive oil
- 3 tbsp white vinegar

- 2 tbsp dried oregano
- 1 tablespoon salt
- 1 ½ tsp ground black pepper
- 5 pounds pork shoulder, trimmed of excess fat

Directions

1. In a mortar and pestle, mix the garlic cloves, olive oil, vinegar, oregano, salt, and black pepper; mash to a paste.
2. Apply a tiny knife to the pork and make deep slices. Put garlic paste within the slices, and then rub the pork with the leftover paste.
3. Put the pork in a roasting pan with a rack after sealing it in a plastic bag. Allow to marinate for 8 to 48 hours in the fridge.
4. Remove the pork from the refrigerator, expose it, and let it sit at room temperature for 1 to 2 hours.
5. Set the oven to 300 degrees Fahrenheit (150 degrees C).
6. For around two hours, roast the pork with the skin side down in a preheated oven. After turning the pork over, roast it for an additional 2 to 4 hours, or until the juices run clear and an instant-read thermometer put into the center registers at least 145 degrees F (63 degrees C).

Cook's Tip:

- If you don't have a mortar and pestle, mash garlic paste with the back of a spoon in a solid basin.

11. COQUITO RECIPE

PREP TIME 10 minutes

COOK TIME 5 hours

ADDITIONAL TIME 4 hours

TOTAL TIME 9 hours 10 minutes

INGREDIENTS

- 1 1/2 cups of rum
- 2 cinnamon sticks
- 4 oz raisins, non-compulsory
- 1 (14 oz) can sweetened condensed milk
- 1 (15 oz) can cream of coconut (Coco Lopez)
- 1 (13.5 oz) can coconut milk (with thick coconut cream on top)
- 4 oz evaporated milk
- 1/2 tsp freshly ground nutmeg
- 1/2 tsp ground cinnamon
- 1/2 tsp vanilla extract
- 4 tbsp shredded coconut, non-compulsory

INSTRUCTIONS

1. Non-compulsory: Mix the rum, cinnamon sticks, and non-compulsory raisins in a sizable pitcher or two sizable jars with lids to make around 56 ounces of liquid (if using). Let sit for a minimum of an hour and a maximum of a week. (Your coquito will have a richer flavor as a result.)
2. Puree all the additional ingredients in a blender. Pour the mixture into the bottle and shake vigorously to incorporate the rum and raisins.
3. Prior to serving, chill for at least 4 hours to allow flavors to mingle and coquito to thicken. (As the coconut cream cools, it will get thicker.)

4. For up to two weeks, keep in the refrigerator in an airtight container. Every time, shake well before serving!

NOTES

- Use high-quality coconut milk with a thick layer of coconut cream on top for this recipe. Your coquito won't be as thick if your canned coconut milk doesn't have a substantial coating of coconut cream on top.
- Goya or Coco Lopez frequently produce coconut cream. Chunks of shredded coconut are mixed into a very thick, sweetened coconut milk. The coconut mentioned as the only ingredient in coconut cream is not the same as this.
- You can use any rum variety that you choose. Although light rum is typically used, dark aged rum or rum with coconut flavoring can also be nice.

12. BASIC COQUITO

Prep Time: 5 mins

Additional Time: 1 hrs

Total Time: 1 hrs 5 mins

Servings: 14

Yield: 1 cup of servings

Ingredients

- ½ tsp ground cinnamon
- 1 (14 ounce) can sweetened condensed milk
- 1 (14 ounce) can cream of coconut, shaken very well before opening
- 1 (14 ounce) can coconut milk, shaken very well before opening
- 1 (12 fluid ounce) can evaporated milk
- 1 ½ cups of rum (such as Bacardi®), or as need

Directions

1. Using a funnel, add cinnamon to a sizable bottle or other container that can hold at least 8 cups of. Through the funnel, add rum, cream of coconut, coconut milk, evaporated milk, and sweetened condensed milk. Stir or shake vigorously to mix.
2. Coquito should be cooled for at least an hour. Before serving, mix or shake.

Culinary Note:

- Use both ordinary and pineapple-flavored rum for an extra-special tropical flavor. The flavor will be similar to a combination between eggnog and pina colada.

13. EASY PINA COLADA FRENCH TOAST

Prep Time: 15 mins

Cook Time: 25 mins

Total Time: 40 mins

Servings: 6

Yield: 12 slices

Ingredients

- 8 eggs
- ⅔ cup of milk
- ½ cup of bottled pina colada drink mix
- 1 tablespoon butter, or as needed
- 12 (1/2 inch thick) slices French bread

- 2 bananas, split

Directions

1. In a bowl, mix the milk, eggs, and pina colada mix. Melt butter in a pan over medium heat until the froth has disappeared. Bread slices should be submerged in the egg mixture and turned over a few times.
2. 2 bread slices should be gently placed into the heated skillet at a time, and the french toast should be pan-fried for about 2 minutes on every side, or until golden brown. While you finish cooking, move the cooked french toast slices to a preheated dish. To serve, place several slices of banana on top of every 2-slice portion.

14. EGGNOG BREAD PUDDING WITH COQUITO SAUCE

Prep Time:10 mins

Cook Time:45 mins

Total Time:55 mins

Servings:10

Yield:1 9x5-inch loaf

Ingredients

- 5 cups of cubed bread
- ¼ cup of raisins
- 2 ¼ cups of eggnog
- 4 large eggs
- ⅓ cup of white sugar
- 1 tsp vanilla extract
- 1 cup of packed brown sugar

- ½ cup of unsalted butter
- ½ cup of heavy cream
- 3 tbsp coconut-flavored rum

Directions

1. Set the oven to 350 degrees Fahrenheit (175 degrees C). A 9x5-inch loaf pan should be buttered.
2. In a bowl, mix the bread and the raisins; pour the mixture into the loaf pan.
3. In a another bowl, mix the eggnog, eggs, white sugar, and vanilla extract. the bread mixture with the liquid.
4. Bake in the preheated oven for 40 to 45 minutes, or until a knife inserted in the center comes out clean.
5. Brown sugar and butter should be melted in a skillet over medium heat. Add the cream and rum, and simmer for about 5 minutes, or until the sauce thickens and is reduced to 1 1/2 cups of. Over the bread pudding, serve warm.

15. GANDULE RICE

PREP TIME 15 mins

COOK TIME 22 mins

ADDITIONAL TIME 30 mins

TOTAL TIME 1 hr 7 mins

INGREDIENTS

- 3 cups of uncooked white rice
- 1 tablespoon achiote oil
- ½ pound bacon
- ½ pound pork tenderloin split into thin, short, narrow strips
- 4 cloves garlic lightly chop up

- ½ green bell pepper diced
- 1 small onion diced
- 1 bunch cilantro lightly chop up
- 5 stalks green onion thinly split
- 3 cups of chicken broth
- 2 packets Sazon Goya
- 1 can 8 ounces tomato sauce
- 1 can 15 ounces gandules verdes, drained
- 1 can 6 ounces pitted black olives, drained

INSTRUCTIONS

1. Cool running water should be used to thoroughly rinse the rice. Drain, then set apart.
2. Turn up the heat to medium-high in a big pan. Add bacon, pork, and achiote oil. Cook for 5 to 10 minutes, or until browned.
3. Garlic, bell pepper, and onion are added next. About 2-3 minutes, or until the onions are transparent and aromatic.
4. then incorporate green onion and cilantro. Heat through while stirring to mix. Turn off the heat and leave the pot alone.
5. Fill the rice cooker with drained rice. Add the tomato sauce, gandule beans, olives, chicken broth, Sazon Goya packets, and tomato sauce.
6. Remove oil from the pork mixture and throw it away. Fill the rice pot with pork. Stir thoroughly to mix.
7. Prepare rice in the rice cooker. Open the rice cooker after it has completed cooking, then fluff the rice by swirling it with a fork.

NOTES

- Close the lid, set the Instant Pot to sealing, and cook the rice setting if using one. It will take 12 minutes to prepare this. Give the pressure 10 minutes to naturally release. Valve should be set to venting. Open the container after the pin has fallen, then fluff the rice by swirling with a fork.
- You can also cook this in the oven or on the stove.

NUTRITION

Serving: 1gCalories: 323kcalCarbs: 43gProtein: 15gFat: 9gSat fat: 3gPolyunSat fat: 6gCholesterol: 34mgSodium: 614mgFiber: 1gSugar: 1g

16. ADOBO SEASONING

prep time: 5 MINUTES

total time: 5 MINUTES

Ingredients

- 1/4 cup of garlic powder
- 2 tbsp salt
- 1 tablespoon black pepper
- 1 tablespoon oregano
- 1 tablespoon ground cumin
- 1 tsp turmeric
- 1 tsp onion powder (non-compulsory)

Instructions

1. Mix everything in a bowl, then seal the container tightly.
2. Suitable Products
3. I make money from eligible purchases as an Amazon Associate and member of other affiliate programs.

Nutrition Information:

YIELD: 30 SERVING SIZE: 1
Amount Per Serving: CALORIES: 6TOTAL FAT: 0gSAT FAT: 0gTRANS FAT: 0gUNSAT FAT: 0gCHOLESTEROL: 0mgSODIUM: 424mgCARBS: 1gFIBER: 0gSUGAR: 0gPROTEIN: 0g

17. HORCHATA DE ARROZ (MEXICAN RICE DRINK)

PREP TIME 20 mins

SOAKING TIME 5 hrs

TOTAL TIME 5 hrs 20 mins

INGREDIENTS

- 1 cup of uncooked white rice (any kind will do)
- 1/4 cup of almonds, chop up
- 2 cinnamon sticks or 2 tsp of cinnamon powder
- 1 can (14 ounces) of condensed milk
- 2 1/2 cups of milk
- 2 tsp vanilla extract
- 3 cups of water 2 cups of for soaking the rice, 1 cup of to add at the end
- Ice, for serving

INSTRUCTIONS

1. the rice in water
2. White uncooked rice, split almonds, and cinnamon sticks (or powder) should all be mixd in a big basin or pot.
3. To ensure that the flavors are distributed evenly, thoroughly mix the mixture with water.
4. Give the mixture at least 5 hours, ideally all night, to soak. Before moving on to the next step, the rice needs to be soft.

5. Mix the mixture with the rice.
6. Blend the contents in a food processor.
7. The mixture should be smooth once all of the rice has been thoroughly ground up in the blender.
8. Once more, filter the resulting liquid into a big pitcher. This will get rid of any large bits.
9. To assist in pressing the juice out of the pulpy, paste-like combination, you might need to use a spatula or spoon.
10. For at least an hour, place it in the refrigerator.
11. Complete the Mexican horchata.
12. Mix the milk, condensed milk, and vanilla essence in a separate bowl.
13. Finally, mix the two mixes in a big jar with 1 cup of water. Before serving this beverage, make sure the ingredients are thoroughly blended.
14. Serve cold Mexican horchata in serving glasses filled with ice and topped with a cinnamon stick. On top, sprinkle some cinnamon powder.

NUTRITION

Serving: 1servingCalories: 222kcalCarbs: 51gProtein: 9gFat: 9gSat fat: 4gPolyunSat fat: 1gMonounSat fat: 3gTrans Fat: 0.001gCholesterol: 26mgSodium: 94mgPotassium: 365mgFiber: 1gSugar: 31gVit. A: 260IUVit. C: 1mgCalcium: 263mgIron: 1mg

18. TRY THESE BELOVED PUERTO RICAN RECIPES

PREP TIME 20 mins

COOK TIME 18 mins

MARINATING TIME 60 mins

TOTAL TIME 98 mins

SERVINGS 4 servings

YIELD 4 sandwiches

Ingredients

- For the marinade and steak
- Juice of 3 medium limes (about 1/3 cup of)
- 1/4 cup of vegetable oil
- 4 cloves garlic, mashed to a paste
- 1 1/2 tbsp adobo (homemade or store-bought)
- 2 tsp onion powder
- 1 tsp dried oregano
- 1 tsp ground cumin
- 1/2 tsp black pepper
- 2 pounds boneless, thin-slice ribeye steaks (about 4 thin-slice steaks)
- For the mayo-ketchup
- 1/2 cup of mayonnaise
- 1/3 cup of ketchup
- Juice of 1 lime (about 1 1/2 tsp)
- 1 tsp granulated garlic
- 3/4 tsp adobo (or kosher salt)
- For the jibarito sandwich
- 4 medium green plantains
- Vegetable oil, for frying plantains
- 4 to 8 slices mozzarella cheese
- Green leaf lettuce leaves
- 1 ripe beefsteak tomato, split
- 1/2 red onion, thinly split in rings

Method

1. Make the marinade for the steak:
2. Lime juice, vegetable oil, garlic paste, adobo, onion powder, oregano, cumin, and black pepper should all be mixd in a quart mason jar. To ensure that the components are thoroughly blended, screw the lid on firmly and shake the jar briskly for 40–1 minute.
3. Pour the marinade into a shallow dish or a strong zip-top food storage bag to marinate the steaks. Flip every ribeye steak to coat it before adding it to the marinade. For at least an hour and up to 12 hours, marinate covered in the fridge.

4. Mayonnaise-ketchup mixture: Whisk the mayonnaise, ketchup, lime juice, granulated garlic, and adobo together in a 1-quart mixing basin until smooth.
5. The mayo-ketchup should be covered and chilled until you're ready to assemble the sandwiches. The mayo-ketchup can be made five days ahead of time and kept in the fridge.

6. Prepare the plantains by sliceting off 1/2 inch of every end to remove the stems, then peeling and chopping them 20 minutes before you intend to grill the steaks. Slice a slit along the length of the plantain's backside using the point of a paring knife. Push up the peel of the plantain using the meaty portion of your thumb.
7. Peel the plantain and then slice it in half lengthwise. The remaining plantains should be repeated.
8. Set up your frying area:
9. 2 inches of vegetable oil should be used in a 12-inch frying pan, which should be heated at medium heat.
10. Prepare a drainage station by setting a cooling rack over a sheet pan or line a sheet pan with paper towels to soak up the frying oil as you wait for the oil to heat.
11. When you're finished frying the tostones, place them in your oven set to "warm."
12. When the oil reveryes 330°F or the handle of a wooden spoon starts to bubble when placed in the oil, it's time to add the four plantain slabs (you'll cook them in two batches).
13. The plantains should be fried for two minutes before being carefully turned over with tongs. Cook the plantains for an additional 2 minutes, or until a knifetip can pass through them without encountering any resistance. Utilizing tongs, remove the plantains from the oil and set them onto the sheet pan to soak up any extra oil.
14. Continue by using the second batch of plantains.
15. Remove the steaks from the refrigerator: Let the steaks sit at room temperature for a few minutes before smashing the plantains.
16. Break apart the plantains:
17. While you smash the plantains, turn up the heat on the oil in the frying pan.
18. Place the slab of plantains on a sliceting board, then cover it with wax or parchment paper. To smash the plantain to a thickness of 1/3 inch, use a heavy pan (a cast iron skillet works best for this).
19. The bottom of the plantain should be removed off the sliceting board using a knife or narrow spatula so that it can be placed back on the rack.
20. The remaining plantains should be flattened by smashing them.

21. Plantains should be fried a second time once the oil in the pan reveryes 350°F (180°C). To do this, return the flattened plantains to the oil. To prevent overcrowding the pan, you will need to work in groups of two or three.
22. The plantains should be fried for 2 minutes on every side, or until the exteriors are crispy and the edges are gently brown.
23. Using a pair of tongs, remove the tostones from the oil and place them on a rack to drain while you continue to fry the other plantains.
24. The sheet pan should be kept heated in the oven once all the tostones have been fried while the steaks are being seared.
25. Heat a 12-inch or bigger skillet over medium-high heat before searing the steaks. Pour one tablespoon of vegetable oil into the pan after heat is visible coming from it.
26. Lay the steaks in the pan gently and press them into the surface with your fingertips or a pair of tongs. An even sear is ensured by this touch. The beef is seared for 4 minutes (for medium-rare). The steaks should be turned over with a pair of tongs and seared for a further 4 minutes.
27. The steaks should rest for five minutes after being taken out of the pan.
28. Put the jibarito sandwiches together:
29. Spread 1 1/2 tbsp of the mayo-ketchup mixture onto every tortilla before assembling the sandwiches. On the bottom of 4 tostones, arrange a slice of cheese, then 1 piece of steak, a leaf of lettuce, 2 slices of tomato, and a few slices of onion. Add another piece of cheese to the top of these before adding the top tostón.
30. Right away serve the jibarito.

19. JOY'S GREEN BANANA SALAD

Ingredients

- 6 small unripe (green) bananas
- 2 tbsp olive oil, separated
- 1 green bell pepper, split into thin rings
- 1 cup of small shrimp - peel off and deveined
- 1 cup of crab meat
- 1 sweet onion, chop up
- 1 pinch salt and pepper as need
- 1 tsp white sugar
- 3/4 cup of red wine vinegar
- 2 slices crisp cooked bacon, crumbled

- 1 hard-cooked egg, peel off and split

Steps

1. Bring water in a big pot to a boil. Bananas should have their ends slice off, and the peel should be slit lengthwise. Cook bananas until they are soft in boiling water (similar to a potato). Drain, let cool, then take off peels. Place in a serving bowl after being slice into small pieces. Over the pieces, drizzle 1 tablespoon of olive oil and swirl to coat.
2. The remaining tablespoon of oil should be heated in a skillet over medium-high heat in the meantime. Fry the crab and shrimp for 5 minutes or until fully cooked. Set apart for cooling.
3. Add shrimp, onions, and green pepper to the bananas in the bowl. Whisk the sugar, red wine vinegar, and bacon bits in a separate basin. Place the bananas in this mixture and gently toss to coat. Add salt and pepper as need. If desired, add slices of hard-boiled egg as a garnish.

20. MAICENA (CORN PUDDING)

Prep Time: 5 mins

Cook Time: 23 mins

Total Time: 28 mins

Servings: 4

Ingredients

- ¼ cup of cornstarch
- 2 cups of milk
- ½ cup of white sugar, or as need
- ½ tsp salt
- 2 egg yolks
- 1 slice lemon rind
- 1 tsp vanilla extract

Directions

1. In a pot, warm cornstarch over medium heat. Slowly stir in the milk. Add salt and sugar. For about 15 minutes, cook and stir until just slightly thickened.
2. In a bowl, whisk egg yolks. Add 1/4 of the cornstarch mixture and stir. Add the egg-cornstarch mixture to the cooking vessel. For about a minute, cook and toss everything together. Add the lemon rind; boil and stir for 7 to 10 minutes, or until thickened. Remove from the heat, then stir in the vanilla extract.

21. MANGO PUDDING (FLAN DE MANGO)

Prep Time:15 mins

Cook Time:45 mins

Total Time:1 hrs

Servings:12

Yield:12 servings

Ingredients

- 1 cup of white sugar
- 1 tablespoon lemon juice
- 2 cups of pureed mango
- 1 (14 ounce) can sweetened condensed milk
- 2 tbsp cornstarch
- 1 tablespoon rum (Non-compulsory)
- 1 cup of evaporated milk
- 6 eggs, beaten
- 1 pinch salt

Directions

1. Set oven to 350 degrees Fahrenheit (175 degrees C). About 1 1/2 inches of water should be added to a big, shallow baking pan.
2. Mix the sugar and lemon juice in an 8x13-inch aluminum baking pan over medium heat. until caramelized, cook and stir. Mango, sweetened condensed milk, cornstarch, rum, evaporated milk, eggs, and salt are added after the mixture has been removed from the heat.
3. Put the pan with the mango mixture into the water-filled pan. Bake for 45 minutes, or until the mixture is solid, in the preheated oven. Before turning out onto a dish, let it cool.

22. PUERTO RICAN MOFONGO

Prep10 MIN

Total20 MIN

Servings4

Ingredients

- 4green plantains
- 1lb of chicharrón (crunchy pork skin)
- 3garlic cloves, mashed
- 4tsp of olive oil
- 2cups of frying oil

Steps

1. Before placing the plantains on the hot skillet with oil, peel them, slice them into 1 1/2-inch slices, soak them in salted water for 15 minutes, drain them, and then pat them dry.

2. Fry them over medium-low heat for approximately 12 minutes, or until they are light brown. Don't forget to rotate them. To make them easier to mash, don't overbrown them. To see if they are finished, pierce them with a fork.
3. Take them out and pound them in a mortar. Add some chop up garlic and chicharrón pieces.
4. Once all of the plantains have been mashed, form them into a half-sphere with your hands or a container. Serve hot with your preferred beef or chicken broth.

23. EASY CHICKEN MOFONGO RECIPE

INGREDIENTS

For the mofongo:

- 4 green plantains
- 1 lb of chicharrón (pork rinds)
- 1 slice bacon, cooked and crumbled
- 3 garlic cloves, mashed
- 4 tsp of olive oil
- 2 cups of frying oil

For the Creole sauce:

- 1 tablespoon butter
- 1 tablespoon extra virgin olive oil
- 1 large clove garlic (chop up)
- 1/4 cup of onions (chop up, about 1/2 medium onion)
- 1/4 cup of green bell pepper (chop up)
- 1/4 cup of yellow or red bell pepper (chop up)
- 1/2 cup of celery (chop up)
- 1/2 tsp paprika
- 1 1/2 tsp Creole seasoning
- 1/2 tsp dried leaf thyme
- 1/2 tsp dried leaf oregano

- 1/2 tsp dried leaf basil
- 1 tsp Worcestershire sauce
- 1/4 tsp hot pepper sauce
- 1/4 tsp freshly ground pepper
- 1 can (14.5 ounces every) diced tomatoes with juice
- 1 can (approximately 1 2/3 cups of) chicken stock (or vegetable stock)
- 4 green onions (split, with most of the green)
- 1 heaping tablespoon tomato paste
- 2 tbsp butter

For the chicken:

- 8 boneless skinless chicken thighs (see notes above if using bone-in, skin-on thighs, which are also just as flavorful in this recipe.)
- 2 tbsp olive oil
- 2 tsp celtic sea salt
- 1 tsp fresh cracked pepper
- 2 tsp garlic powder
- 1 tsp lemon juice

Hands Free Mode:

- Prevent screen from sleeping

INSTRUCTIONS

1. The Mofongo:
2. In a sizable pot or Dutch oven, heat the oil.
3. Plantains should be peel off, slice into 1 1/2-inch slices, and soaked in salty water for 15 minutes while the oil heats up.
4. Before placing them in the heated pot with oil, remove plantains from the water and pat them dry with a paper towel. Make certain that all water has been dried entirely.
5. Plantains should be fried in tiny batches for 12 minutes at medium-low heat, or until they are a very light brown color.
6. While cooking, be sure to turn the plantains.
7. Plaintains shouldn't be overly browned because you want them to remain tender and easy to mash; instead, they should have a wonderful dark yellow and light brown color to feel soft to the touch. Use a fork to check whether the food is done.

8. Plantains should be removed from the oil and placed in a big bowl or mortar.
9. With a pestle or the back of a spoon, crush plantains.
10. Smash some bacon crumbles, crushed garlic, and chunks of pork rind into the potatoes.
11. Once all of the plantains have been mashed, make 8 circles by hand-forming every one into a circle or half-circle.
12. The Chicken:
13. All ingredients should be mixd in a bowl or plastic bag and let to marinate for up to a day.
14. A 400 degree oven is recommended.
15. Use parchment paper to cover a baking sheet.
16. Cook chicken thighs on the outside in a hot pan until slightly golden brown as an non-compulsory step. (Reduce the overall cooking time by 5-8 minutes if pre-browning.)
17. Chicken thighs should not be too closely spaced apart when they are placed on parchment paper.
18. After 10 minutes, flip the pan over and take the temperature. Check the temperature of the chicken after 10 more minutes of baking.
19. When the chicken reveryes around 150 degrees, turn the broiler to high and crisp it for about 5 minutes, or until the internal temperature reveryes 165 degrees.
20. Applied to the creole sauce:
21. A medium pot is used to heat the butter and oil.
22. Garlic, onions, peppers, and celery should all be chop up. The vegetables should be sautéed for 5 to 7 minutes, or until just tender.
23. In the meantime, mix the Worcestershire sauce, spicy sauce, basil, oregano, thyme, paprika, Creole spice, and ground pepper in a small cup of.
24. Add the seasoning combination after stirring the tomatoes into the vegetables. Sauté for an additional minute.
25. Put stock, either chicken or vegetable, in and bring to a boil. Add the green onions, slice into slices.
26. To the pot, add cooked chicken.
27. Boiling should go on without cover for 10 minutes. The liquid will cook off in large amounts.
28. Add the tomato paste and butter and stir until the sauce is well-mixd.
29. Serve right away over mofongo in a big, deep bowl or dish.

24. MY CLASSIC PUERTO RICAN CARNE GUISADA

Prep Time:15 mins

Cook Time:1 hrs 30 mins

Total Time:1 hrs 45 mins

Servings:4

Yield:4 servings

Ingredients

- 1 ½ tbsp corn oil
- 2 pounds beef round steak, slice into serving-size pieces
- 3 cloves cloves garlic, crushed
- ½ tsp ground black pepper
- ½ tsp dried oregano
- ½ cup of dry white wine
- 2 tbsp sofrito
- 1 tablespoon salt
- 1 cube beef bouillon
- 3 bay leaves
- 3 potatoes, peel off and cubed
- 3 carrots, peel off and chop up
- 1 ½ tbsp Spanish olives
- 1 tablespoon tomato paste

Directions

1. In a skillet with medium to high heat, heat the oil, then brown the meat for about 10 minutes on every side. In a mortar, mix oregano, pepper, and garlic to crush.

2. Fill the skillet with steak and wine. Stir everything together, then add the sofrito, salt, beef bouillon cube, and bay leaves. Bring to a boil. Cook the beef for about an hour on low heat with the lid on. When the meat still can't be easily penetrated with a fork, add 1/2 cup of water and continue cooking.
3. Add the tomato paste, olives, potatoes, and carrots. About 20 minutes, cook over low heat until the veggies are tender and the sauce has thickened.

Cook's Notes:

- You can use red or white wine in this dish, and when you add the carrots and potatoes, add 1/2 cup of sweet peas as well.
- For my Carne Guisada, I used a sofrito recipe from this source and served it with rice.

25. PASTELES WITH YUCA AND PLANTAINS

Prep Time:55 mins

Cook Time:1 hrs 23 mins

Total Time:2 hrs 18 mins

Ingredients

- 2 pounds yuca, peel off and coarsely chop up
- 2 pounds green plantains, peel off and coarsely chop up
- 2 pounds yautia, peel off and coarsely chop up
- 2 cups of milk
- 1 pound lard
- 1 pound achiote seeds
- 1 tablespoon olive oil, or as need
- 1 onion, chop up
- 1 green bell pepper, chop up
- 2 pounds pork shoulder roast, slice into small cubes

- 1 pound ham, slice into small cubes
- 2 cups of garbanzo beans
- 2 (8 ounce) cans tomato sauce
- 1 (5 ounce) jar pitted Spanish olives
- 1 (4 ounce) jar capers
- 3 tbsp orange juice
- 4 sprigs cilantro, chop up
- 2 tbsp dried oregano
- 1 tablespoon salt
- 2 cloves garlic, chop up
- 24 plantain leaves
- kitchen string

Directions

1. Blend the milk, yuca, green plantains, yautia, and other ingredients into a thick mixture that resembles oatmeal.
2. In a saucepan over medium-low heat, mix the achiote seeds and lard; cook for about 5 minutes, or until the fat is melted and crimson in color. Remove the achiote seeds. Mix the yuca paste with half of the lard.
3. In a big pot, warm up the olive oil over medium heat. Cook and toss the onion and green bell pepper for about 5 minutes, or until they are soft. When the pork is no longer pink in the center, around 8 to 10 minutes, add the ham, garbanzo beans, tomato sauce, olives, capers, orange juice, cilantro, oregano, salt, and garlic. Cook and stir throughout this time. Get rid of the heat.
4. Mix the pork mixture with 2/3 of the remaining fat.
5. Spread a little of the leftover grease on every plantain leaf. Every one should have a huge dollop of yuca paste in the center, followed by a scoop of the pork mixture. To make a rectangle pastel, fold up the sides of every leaf to contain the filling.
6. 2 pasteles should be stacked and tied together with kitchen string. With the remaining pasteles, repeat.
7. Bring water in a big pot to a boil. Put pasteles in. Cook for about an hour, or until the filling is soft. Pastels must be opened before serving.

26. PASTELÓN (SWEET PLANTAIN LASAGNA)

Prep Time 40 minutes

Cook Time 30 minutes

Total Time 1 hour 10 minutes

Ingredients

- 6-7 very ripe plantains almost all black
- Mazola Corn Oil for air frying and greasing the pan
- 1 recipe's worth of picadillo
- 1 cup of shredded part-skim mozzarella cheese
- 2 eggs beaten

Instructions

1. Set the oven to 375 degrees Fahrenheit.
2. Slice every of the plantains into 5–6 pieces after peeling them like you would a banana.
3. Air fry them at 350 degrees for 15 minutes, or until they are thoroughly cooked and caramelized, after brushing with Mazola corn oil. With the back of a plate, press the cooked plantains into a flat surface.
4. Slices of the cooked sweet plantain should be placed on the bottom of a 9" × 9" baking dish that has been greased with corn oil. 1/4 of the mozzarella cheese and half of the turkey picadillo should be added.
5. Repeat the process with another layer of plantains, pork, and cheese, reserving the last 1/2 cup of. Add a final layer of plantains on top.
6. Add the remaining cheese on top, then cover with the beaten eggs. To disperse the eggs, back and forth tilt the pan.

7. Bake the pastelón for 20 to 30 minutes at 375 degrees F, or until the egg is set and the top is frothy and golden brown.
8. Prior to sliceting into and serving the pastelon, give it 15 minutes to chill.

27. PUERTO RICAN STUFFED PEPPERS

Prep Time: 15 minutes

Cook Time: 25 minutes

Total Time: 40 minutes

Ingredients

Puerto Rican Salsa Criolla

- 1 tbsp vegetable oil
- 28 ounces crushed tomato or tomato puree sauce
- 2 tbsp sofrito homemade or store bought is fine
- 1/4 cup of white wine
- 1/2 cup of onions chop up
- 1/2 cup of peppers chop up
- 1 bay leaf
- 3 garlic cloves chop up
- 1/2 tsp oregano
- 1/4 tsp cumin
- 4 tbsp fresh cilantro chop up
- salt and pepper as need

For Meat Filling

- 1 pound ground meat
- 3 bell peppers rinsed, slice horizontally and seeds removed
- 1/2 cup of cooked white or yellow rice
- 6 ounces tomato sauce
- 1/2 cup of white onions chop up
- 1/2 cup of green bell pepper or whatever pepper you have
- 2 tbsp sofrito homemade or store bought is fine

- 2 garlic cloves chop up
- 1 packet Sazon with Annatto found in the Spanish or Latin section of grocery store (I use Goya brand)
- 1/2 tsp oregano
- 1/4 tsp cumin
- 2-3 tbsp fresh cilantro chop up
- salt and pepper as need
- Other Ingredients for Puerto Rican Stuffed Peppers
- Monterey Jack or Mozzarella cheese shredded
- 8 pimiento stuffed green olives (non-compulsory) slice in half and added to meat mixture

Instructions

1. Turn the oven on to 350 degrees.
2. Criolla Salsa Puerto Rican
3. In a medium-sized pot over medium heat, mix the oil, chop up onions, peppers, sofrito, garlic, oregano, cumin, and bay leaf.
4. Until onion is transparent, stir and simmer.
5. Tomato sauce, white wine, cilantro, and salt and pepper as need should also be added.
6. flame to a medium low setting. Cook for 20–25 minutes while stirring.
7. Midway through cooking, stir.
8. Put out the flame. Sauce is finished.
9. For Filling Meat
10. Over medium heat, add ground beef to the pan.
11. Using a wooden spoon or spatula, shred ground beef.
12. Stirring often, brown the ground beef.
13. If the meat is very oily, drain the extra oil from it with a strainer.
14. Mix well the ground meat with the peppers, onions, and garlic.
15. around 5 minutes of cooking.
16. Tomato sauce, sofrito, sazon, oregano, and cumin should be added.
17. Cook for 3 minutes while stirring.
18. Mix the rice and the meat thoroughly before adding.
19. Stir the meat, then add the cilantro. For 10 minutes, cook.
20. Getting the Peppers Ready
21. Peppers should be rinsed and slice horizontally in half.

22. Delete the seeds.
23. Put the peppers in a pan deep enough to hold the sauce topping or an oven-safe baking dish.
24. Fill every pepper cavity with with meat.
25. The remaining sauce should encircle the stuffed peppers after being spooned on top of the peppers.
26. Shredded mozzarella or Monterey jack cheese should be added to the tops.
27. Place a lid on top.
28. Depending on how done you want your peppers, bake them in the oven for 25 to 35 minutes.
29. Serve right away with more sauce on top from the pan.

Notes

Simply omit the cilantro from the recipe if you dislike it.

Nutrition

Serving: 6g | Calories: 531kcal | Carbs: 20g | Protein: 29g | Fat: 35g | Sat fat: 15g | Cholesterol: 107mg | Sodium: 410mg | Potassium: 1038mg | Fiber: 5g | Sugar: 11g | Vit. A: 4210IU | Vit. C: 201.4mg | Calcium: 64mg | Iron: 4.5mg

28. PIÑA COLADA SORBET

YIELD: 6 -8 SERVINGS

PREP TIME: 15 MINS

COOK TIME: 2 HRS

TOTAL TIME: 2 HRS 15 MINS

INGREDIENTS

- 1 fresh pineapple, cubed
- 1 cup of light canned coconut milk
- 2/3 cup of granulated sugar
- Juice of a lime
- 2 tbsp dark rum

- ½ tsp coconut extract, non-compulsory

INSTRUCTIONS

1. Blend every ingredient in a blender together until completely smooth.
2. Put the mixture in the fridge and let it chill.
3. If the mixture has separated, whisk it before adding it to the ice cream machine.
4. As directed by the manufacturer, freeze the sorbet.
5. Until you're ready to serve, keep the sorbet in the freezer in an airtight container that is freezer safe.

NOTES

Freeze the sorbet for a few hours before serving for best results.

NUTRITION

SERVING: 0G, CALORIES: 203KCAL, CARBS: 43G, PROTEIN: 0G, FAT: 2G, SAT FAT: 2G, CHOLESTEROL: 0MG, SODIUM: 29MG, POTASSIUM: 164MG, FIBER: 2G, SUGAR: 37 G, VIT. A: 90IU, VIT. C: 73.6MG, CALCIUM: 20MG, IRON: 0.4MG

29. PIQUE - PUERTO RICAN HOT SAUCE - RECIPE

Prep Time: 5 minutes

Cook Time: 2 days

Total Time: 2 days 5 minutes

Ingredients

- 12 small chili peppers/About 4 ounces – I used a variety of 7-Pots Ajis Pineapples, and Muranga Reds
- 2 cloves garlic slightly crushed
- 10 black peppercorns
- 4 cilantro stems
- Squeeze of lime juice
- White vinegar to fill the jar about a half cup of or so

Instructions

1. Take the pepper stem off. Slice the peppers into pieces that will fit in the jar or container you're using, such as halves or quarters.
2. Put the peppers inside a bottle or jar that holds 8 ounces.
3. Add the lime juice, cilantro stems, cloves, and peppercorns.
4. Vinegar should be poured into the container until it is nearly full, leaving some headspace.
5. Cap it off and shake it vigorously.
6. To let the heat and flavor develop, let it sit out for anything between two days and two weeks. Add extra vinegar and peppers as necessary.

Notes

- Shake it all over the place.
- Heat Index: High (depending on the peppers used).

30. POLLO (CHICKEN) FRICASSEE FROM PUERTO RICO

Prep Time: 40 mins

Cook Time: 6 hrs

Total Time: 6 hrs 40 mins

Servings: 4

Ingredients

- 1 pound chicken drumsticks
- 1 tablespoon adobo seasoning
- ½ (.18 ounce) packet sazon seasoning
- ½ tsp salt
- 5 large red potatoes, peel off and thickly split
- 1 large red bell pepper, seeded and chop up
- 1 large green bell pepper, seeded and chop up
- 1 large onion, chop up
- 5 cloves garlic, chop up
- 1 bunch fresh cilantro, chop up
- 2 tbsp olive oil
- ½ cup of dry red wine
- 1 tsp ground cumin
- 1 tsp dried oregano
- 2 fresh or dried bay leaves

Directions

1. Place the cleaned, dried chicken in a big bowl. Add salt, sazon seasoning, and adobo seasoning to the food. Put the legs in a slow cooker with the potato pieces on top.
2. Blend in a blender the red pepper, green pepper, onion, garlic, cilantro, wine, cumin, and oregano. Add the bay leaves and pour over the chicken.

3. Cook the chicken on Low for 6 to 8 hours, or until it easily comes off the bone.

31. POLVARONES

Prep Time:15 mins

Cook Time:16 mins

Total Time:31 mins

Servings:36

Yield:36 servings

Ingredients

- ½ cup of white sugar
- ½ cup of butter
- ½ cup of shortening
- 1 tablespoon almond extract
- 2 ½ cups of all-purpose flour
- 2 tbsp colored sugar, or as desired (Non-compulsory)
- 2 tbsp sprinkles, or as desired (Non-compulsory)
- 2 tbsp guava paste, or as desired (Non-compulsory)

Directions

1. Set oven to 350 degrees Fahrenheit (175 degrees C).
2. Using an electric mixer, mix white sugar, butter, and shortening in a bowl and beat until creamy. Add almond extract and blend. Batch-adding the flour while vigorously kneading the dough.
3. Place dough balls on baking sheets 2 inches apart, every the size of a walnut. Using the handle of a wooden spoon, make a well in every cookie. Fill the wells with guava paste, sprinkles, and colored sugar.
4. Bake for 16 to 20 minutes in a preheated oven, or until lightly brown.

32. PONCHE DE RON DE PUERTO RICO (COQUITO)

Ingredientes

- 1 taza de agua
- 12 clavos
- 2 ramas de canela
- 1 pedazo de jengibre fresco de 1 pulgada, pelado
- 1 lata (15 onzas) de crema de coco
- 1 lata (12 onzas líquidas) de leche evaporada NESTLÉ CARNATION Evaporated Milk
- 1 taza de ron
- Canela en polvo (opcional)

Directions

1. Put the water, the clams, the canela branch tips, and the jingle in a small container and set it to simmer over a medium flame. Fire-retardant clothing; cuffs. Refresh for fifteen minutes. Remove the canela, the locks, and the jengibre pedant.
2. Place the coconut cream, evaporated milk, ron, and special water in the blender; blend. Liquify for 30 seconds or until the mixture is well blended. Refrigerate in a glass container or bottle for at least two hours or until it is well chilled. Work hard before serving.
3. Serving instructions: Divide 2 onzas among cocktail cups of. If you want it with a canela in mud, Roca.

Notes

- Advice: Add a canela rama inside the coquito bottle to give it more flavor.

33. NATILLA (PUERTO RICAN CUSTARD DESSERT)

Prep Time 5 minutes

Cook Time 15 minutes

Cooling Time 4 hours

Total Time 4 hours 20 minutes

Ingredients

- 2 cups of whole dairy milk
- 2 tbsp corn starch
- 4 egg yolks
- 1/2 cup of granulated sugar
- 2 2 inch pieces of lemon peel
- 1 whole cinnamon stick
- 1/8 tsp salt
- 1 tsp vanilla extract
- ground cinnamon for garnish

Instructions

1. Dissolve the corn starch in 1/2 cup of milk in a sauce pan. Add the remaining milk, eggs, sugar, cinnamon stick, lemon peel, and salt. Mix by whisking.
2. To keep the mixture from curdling, cook it over medium heat while stirring often.
3. Cook for 10 to 15 minutes, or until the mixture thickens and the back of a wooden spoon can be drawn across it.
4. Remove the cinnamon stick and lemon peel after turning off the heat. Add the vanilla essence by whisking.
5. Four ramekins of equal sizes should receive the mixture. For at least 4 hours, cover with plastic wrap and place in the refrigerator.
6. Remove the plastic wrap before serving, then sift some ground cinnamon over the natillas' exterior.

34. PUERTO RICAN CABBAGE, AVOCADO, AND CARROT SALAD

Ingredients

- ½ tsp olive oil
- ½ tsp lime juice
- ½ carrot, shredded
- ½ cup of shredded cabbage
- 4 slices Hass avocado

Directions

- In a bowl, mix the lime juice and olive oil and whisk. Add the carrots and cabbage and toss to coat. Salad should be gently tossed with avocado slices.

Nutrition Facts

serving: 1 serving

calories: 234.9 kcal

Carbs: 15.4 g

protein: 3.1 g

Sat fat: 2.9 g

sodium: 35.8 mg

fiber: 9.8 g

sugar: 3.4 g

35. COQUITO | PUERTO RICAN COCONUT NOG

PREP TIME 10 minutes

COOK TIME 1 minute

INACTIVE TIME 1 hour 39 minutes

TOTAL TIME 1 hour 50 minutes

ingredients

- 1 (12 oz) can evaporated milk
- 1 (14 oz) can sweetened condensed milk
- 2 cups of (1 15 oz can) cream of coconut (like Coco Lopez)
- 1/4 tsp cinnamon
- 1/8 tsp nutmeg
- 1 tsp vanilla
- 1 1/2 cup of white rum
- cinnamon sticks for garnish
- Hands Free Mode:
- Prevent screen from sleeping

instructions

1. Blend all components thoroughly at high speed.
2. Refrigerate for no less than one hour.
3. Shake vigorously before using.
4. Serve in a small glass while cool. Add a cinnamon stick as garnish.
5. notes
6. Coquito (without the egg) will keep for 4-6 months in a refrigerator when stored in an airtight container.
7. Give it a thorough shake before serving and let it sit on the counter for 10 minutes if any of the coconut fat solidifies.

8. In order to make a non-alcoholic version, replace the rum with coconut milk and, as need, rum essence.

36. PUERTO RICAN EMPANADAS

Prep Time 10 mins

Cook Time 45 mins

Total Time 55 mins

Ingredients

Empanada Dough (or use Goya discos)

- 2 ½ cups of All purpose flour + more for sprinkling
- 1 stick butter
- 1 egg beaten
- ¼ cup of water
- 1 pinch salt

Empanada Filling

- 1 pound ground beef
- 1 medium potato parboiled, peel off, and diced small
- ¼ cup of Goya Sofrito + 2 additional Tbsp
- 1 8 oz. can tomato sauce
- 1 packet Goya Sazón con Azafran
- 20 Spanish olives roughly chop up
- ¼ cup of Water
- 1 tsp salt
- ½ cup of Monterey Jack cheese shredded

Instructions

1. To a food processor, add 2 12 cups of AP flour, 1 stick of cold, cubed butter, 1 egg, 14 cup of cold water, and a dash of salt.

2. When the mixture resembles coarse crumbs, pulse it.
3. Onto a piece of plastic wrap, pour the dough mixture. Use your hands to roll the mixture into a ball.
4. Place the dough ball in the refrigerator for 30 minutes after carefully wrapping it in plastic wrap.
5. Remove the dough from the fridge after 30 minutes. Flour should be strewn over a tidy surface. Use a floured rolling pin to make the dough as thin as you can.
6. Place a round bowl or plate measuring 5 to 6 inches atop the dough. Slice a round disc off of the bowl's edge by sliceting along the bowl's edges. Take out the dough circle and reserve it.
7. Continue by using the remaining dough. To slice the remaining dough rounds, the dough must be rolled out again and molded into a ball.
8. Continue sliceting the dough into rounds until it is completely done.
9. A medium potato should be parboiled for 7 to 10 minutes before being peel off and slice into small pieces. 20 Spanish olives are chop up.
10. Add ground beef to a big skillet that's been heated to medium. Cook well, breaking it up as it cooks. When you're done cooking, drain any extra fat. To the pan, add the potato, sofrito, and 1/4 cup of water.
11. Stirring frequently to keep the potatoes from sticking, cook for 10 minutes. 1 Sazon con Azafron seasoning packet, 1/4 cup of water, and a dash of salt should all be added.
12. Stirring often, cook for a further 5 minutes. Stir after adding the olives to the pan.
13. turn the oven on to 350 degrees. Use parchment paper to cover a baking sheet.
14. The pastry rounds should be put on a spotless surface. About 2 Tbsp of the meat filling should be spooned into a pastry round. Sprinkle some Monterey Jack cheese on top. Apply a little water to the pastry round's edges and rub them together.
15. Pull one side of the pastry over the other, then use your fingers to press the edges together. With your fingers or a fork, pinch the edges together after sealing them firmly.
16. The pastry circles should not be overstuffed or they will shatter when baking. The remaining pastry rounds should be repeated.
17. Apply cooking spray to a baking sheet or sheets. On every pan, distribute half of the empanadas. Bake for 25 to 30 minutes, or until the dough is golden brown, in the pan(s). You can bake them in two batches or in two different pans. Enjoy after serving!

Notes

- Using refrigerate Goya discos from your grocery store's refrigerate foods area can replace creating your own dough. Before making the empanadas, make sure to defrost for at least 30 minutes.
- Do not neglect to parboil the potatoes. This crucial step will ensure that your potatoes are cooked just right for the filling!

Nutrition

Serving: 1g | Calories: 298kcal | Carbs: 21g | Fat: 18g | Sat fat: 8g | Cholesterol: 64mg | Sodium: 477mg

37. PUERTO RICAN ROAST PORK SHOULDER (PERNIL)

yield: 18 SERVINGS

prep time: 35 MINUTES

cook time: 5 HOURS

additional time: 2 DAYS

total time: 2 DAYS 5 HOURS 35 MINUTES

Ingredients

- 10 pound pork shoulder, skin-on, bone-in (picnic shoulder)
- 1/2 cup of white vinegar
- 2 large garlic heads, peel off and grated or crushed
- 1/3 cup of Sofrito (red or green)
- 2 tbsp Adobo seasoning
- 2 tbsp dried oregano leaves
- 2 tbsp onion powder
- 1-1/2 tbsp Sazón (3 packets)

- 2 tbsp cumin powder
- 1/2 tbsp Kosher salt
- 1 tsp black pepper

Instructions

1. To prepare the pork shoulder, carefully slice across the front where the skin and fat converge. Create a pocket between the skin and the flesh by sliceting only a few inches on every side and gently pulling and lifting the skin.
2. Make a few small slices into the pork's flesh after pulling back the skin a bit. Avoid sliceting the skin.
3. Make a few slices into the bottom of the pork after turning it over.
4. Put the pork shoulder in a sizable bowl and cover it with vinegar. Rub it all over the meat, making sure to get beneath the skin. Don't use water to wash the vinegar off.
5. While making the paste, arrange the pork on a big dish and reserve.
6. Grated garlic, sofrito, adobo spice, oregano leaves, onion powder, cumin, salt, and black pepper should all be mixd in a small basin. Make a thick paste by stirring.
7. Fill the space between the skin and the flesh with 1/3 of the paste. Massage it into the flesh and slices.
8. A further third of the paste should be rubbed into the slices and the bottom of the pork after turning it over.
9. Use the last third of the paste to rub into the sides of the pork after flipping it over, skin side up.
10. Pull the plastic wrap tightly around the pork and completely enclose it. The box is then placed on a dish after being completely wrapped in aluminum foil. Put the ingredients in the fridge to marinate for up to 3 days.
11. Remove the pork shoulder from the refrigerator and roast it. Remove the foil and plastic wrap, then wipe the paste from the pork skin's top. Allow the pork to rest for 30 minutes after patting the skin dry with a paper towel.
12. Oven: 350 degrees Fahrenheit Place the oven rack in the lower third of the oven.
13. Spray non-stick oil inside a sizable roasting pan and insert a roasting rack. Apply non-stick oil to a sizable sheet of foil. Put the pork on the roasting rack, then wrap the pan in foil that has been lightly greased.
14. The pork shoulder should be roasted for five hours or until it reveryes an internal temperature of 175°F to 205°F. If you want to slice the pork, roast it to 175°F to 180°F; if you want to shred it, cook it to 200°F to 205°F.

15. After removing the foil, take the pan out of the oven. Return the roast to the oven, raising the temperature to 425°F, to crisp and blister the skin. To ensure that the skin is evenly browned, crisped, and blistered, keep an eye on it and turn it every few minutes.
16. The roast should be removed and given 30 minutes to rest.
17. When it's time to serve, separate the flesh from the crispy pig skin by breaking or slicing it into pieces. Place the pork shoulder on a dish, then slice it into pieces or shred it.

Notes

- The vinegar wash aids in breaking down the pork shoulder's brittle connective tissue.
- Most neighborhood grocery stores sell sazón, a Puerto Rican herb flavoring base, in the international foods section. Blend equal parts of ground coriander, cumin, garlic powder, and onion powder if you can't locate it.
- A mixture of Latin or Spanish spices called adobo is used as a general-purpose condiment.
- To infuse flavor into the meat, tightly wrap the pork in plastic wrap.
- After 8 hours and up to 3 days of marinating, the pork can be roasted. The flavor improves with marinating time.
- When the pig is ready to roast, brush off the spice mixture to prevent charring during roasting.
- To prevent the foil from sticking you the pig skin, make sure to spray some oil on it.
- Transferring the pork to a clean pan or rack for the final crisping of the skin is preferable because doing so will prevent excessive smoke from arising from the increased temperature.
- Calculate the amount of time needed to roast pork shoulders of various sizes at 350°F for 35 minutes per pound, until the internal temperature reveryes 180°F. (5 pounds = 3, 7 pounds = 4, and 10 pounds = 6 hours)
- If you want the pork to shred like pulled pork, cook it until it reveryes 200°F to 205°F. If you wish to slice the pork, 175° to 180°F is the ideal range.

Nutrition Information:

YIELD: 18 SERVING SIZE: 1
Amount Per Serving: CALORIES: 753TOTAL FAT: 55gSAT FAT: 20gTRANS FAT: 0gUNSAT FAT: 29gCHOLESTEROL: 227mgSODIUM: 217mgCARBS: 2gFIBER: 0gSUGAR: 0gPROTEIN: 59g

38. PUERTO RICAN SANCOCHO

PREP TIME 40 mins

COOK TIME 2 hrs 30 mins

TOTAL TIME 3 hrs 10 mins

INGREDIENTS

- 1 med yuca
- 1 med white yautia taro root
- 1 green plantain
- 1 yellow sweet plantain
- 10 oz calabaza pumpkin or kabocha squash
- 2 fresh ears sweet corn
- 1 lb pork or beef stew meat trimmed of excess fat and slice into 2-inch pieces
- 1 lb boneless chicken thighs trimmed of excess fat and slice into 2-inch pieces
- 1 ½ tbsp salt + more as need
- ¼ tsp black pepper
- 1 tbsp olive oil + more as needed
- ½ cup of sofrito
- 10 cups of pork or beef stock
- 3 dried bay leaves
- 1 cup of Spanish chorizo thinly split
- white rice for serving

INSTRUCTIONS

1. The yuca, yautia, green plantain, and yellow plantain should all be peel off and split into 1-inch pieces.
2. One medium yuca, one medium white yautia, one green plantain, and one sweet plantain

3. Slice the calabaza into 1-inch pieces with the skin still on after removing the seeds.
4. Calabaza, 10 oz.
5. While you prepare the remaining ingredients for the soup, place every component in a separate bowl, covering the veggies with water to prevent them from browning.
6. The corn should be husked before being slice into 2-inch-thick pieces. Place aside.
7. 2 new sweet corn ears
8. Chicken and pork (or beef) should be season with 1/4 tsp of black pepper and 1/2 tablespoon of salt.
9. 1 pound of beef or pork stew meat, 1 pound of boneless chicken thighs, and 1/4 tsp of black pepper
10. In a big pot, heat 1 tablespoon of oil on medium-high. For five minutes, add the pork and brown it on all sides.
11. Then add the chicken to the same pot and brown on both sides for a further 5 minutes, adding oil as required if the pot becomes dry. Using a slotted spoon, remove to a clean, big bowl. Use a slotted spoon to transfer to the same bowl as the meat.
12. 1 tablespoon of olive oil
13. Sofrito is added to the pot while the heat is reduced to medium, and any browned meat flakes are scraped out and mixed in. Cook the mixture for 5 to 7 minutes, or until the liquid has evaporated and the mixture has turned dark.
14. 12 cup of salsa
15. Add the chicken, pork, and any remaining liquids to the pot. Over high heat, add the stock, bay leaves, and last tablespoon of salt. Bring to a boil.
16. ten cups of beef or pork stock, three dried bay leaves
17. Once it begins to simmer, lower the heat to medium-low, cover the pan, and cook for 15 minutes while stirring regularly.
18. Every vegetable should be added in order of firmness, cooking for 5 minutes after every addition to prevent the vegetables from disintegrating.
19. Start with the yuca and simmer it for 30 minutes before adding the yautia, green plantain, yellow plantain, calabaza, and corn.
20. Stir thoroughly to incorporate the chorizo before adding. Cook the beef and veggies for a further 10 to 15 minutes over medium-low heat, or until they are soft and readily fall apart with a fork.
21. 1 cup of chorizo spanish
22. Serve with white rice or fresh bread as a side dish and adjust salt as need.
23. is white rice

39. PUERTO RICAN-STYLE SHEPHERD'S PIE

Ingredients

- 2 tsp kosher salt
- 4 ripe plantains (yellow with black spots), peel off and halved crosswise
- 3 tbsp salted butter, + more for the pan
- 3 tbsp olive oil
- 1 pound ground beef
- 1 tsp adobo seasoning
- 1 medium onion, diced
- 1 small green bell pepper, diced
- 1/2 tsp ground cumin
- 1/2 tsp paprika (preferably smoked)
- 1/2 tsp dried oregano
- 1 cup of tomato sauce
- 1/3 cup of pimento-stuffed green olives, split
- 2 tsp capers (non-compulsory)
- 2 large eggs, beaten
- 1¼ cups of shredded Monterey Jack, mozzarella or cheddar cheese

Preparation

1. Salting some water in a medium pot, bring to a boil over high heat. About 15 minutes after adding the plantains, start simmering them. Add the 3 tbsp of butter to a bowl with the plantains, and mash until smooth. Separate the mixture.
2. Set your oven to 400 degrees. Set aside the buttered medium baking dish.
3. In a large skillet over medium-high heat, warm the olive oil. When the beef is brown, add it along with the adobo seasoning and simmer, breaking up the meat with a wooden spoon. Transfer the meat to a bowl after removing it from the pan. Reduce heat to medium and toss in the pepper, onion, cumin, paprika, and oregano for about 6 minutes, or until the onion is transparent. beef back into the skillet. When the liquid has evaporated, add the tomato sauce, olives, and capers and simmer, stirring occasionally. Get rid of the heat.

4. Spread the beef mixture in the bottom of the baking dish to start assembling the casserole. Then, layer the plantains on top of the eggs and beef mixture. Add the cheese on top. Bake the cheese uncovered for 30 to 40 minutes, or until it turns golden brown. Serve hot.

40. PUERTO RICAN STEAMED RICE

Prep Time:10 mins

Cook Time:25 mins

Total Time:35 mins

Servings:8

Ingredients

- 3 cups of water
- 2 tbsp vegetable oil
- 1 tsp salt
- 2 cups of uncooked calrose rice, rinsed

Directions

1. Over high heat, bring water, oil, and salt to a boil in a pot.
2. When the water has almost completely evaporated, add the rice and stir. Medium-low heat should be used. Cook for 20 to 25 minutes with a cover on.
3. Serve after another stir. It's possible that rice will be a touch sticky and adhere to the pot's bottom.

41. RISOTTO WITH PIGEON PEAS AND PULLED PORK (RISOTTO CON GANDULES Y PERNIL)

Ingredients

- 2 pounds pork shoulder roast, slice into chunks
- salt and ground black pepper as need
- 3 tbsp extra-virgin olive oil, separated
- 8 cups of chicken stock, separated
- 1 (15 ounce) can pigeon peas, drained and rinsed
- ½ onion, lightly chop up
- ¾ cup of arborio rice
- ½ cup of grated Parmesan cheese

Directions

1. Use salt and pepper to season the meat.
2. In a big pot, heat 2 tbsp of oil to medium-high heat. Add the pork and cook for 2 minutes on every side, or until browned. Add two cups of chicken stock. For about an hour or until the pork is soft to the fork, reduce heat to low, cover, and simmer. With a fork, shred and then move to a plate.
3. Set the pot's remaining 1 tablespoon oil to medium heat. Cook and stir for 2 minutes after adding the onion and pigeon peas. Add arborio rice and stir. Just cover the rice with chicken stock before cooking and stirring the rice until it absorbs it. Continue adding stock and stirring frequently for about 20 minutes, or until every addition is absorbed and the rice is cooked but still firm to the biting.
4. Mix the rice with the chop up meat. On top, grate some Parmesan cheese.

Nutrition Facts

serving: 4 servings

calories: 625.7 kcal

Carbs: 52.5 g

protein: 39.4 g

Sat fat: 8.7 g

cholesterol: 109.3 mg

sodium: 1941.3 mg

fiber: 4.4 g

sugar: 1.7 g

42. SLOW COOKED PUERTO RICAN PORK (PERNIL)

PREP TIME 1 day

COOK TIME 8 hours

TOTAL TIME 1 day 8 hours

ingredients

- 4 lb pork shoulder or pork butt
- 6 garlic cloves, pressed
- 1/4 tsp ground black pepper
- 1 tablespoon oregano
- 1 1/2 tbsp olive oil
- 1 1/2 tbsp white vinegar
- 4 tsp salt

instructions

1. Olive oil, pepper, oregano, vinegar, salt, and all of the above are mixd. Garlic mixture over meat; chill for at least 4 hours or overnight.

2. When ready, place in crockpot and cook on low for 8 hours.
3. Done! Consume fervently.

notes

- The pork should be cooked in the crockpot without any liquid. Pork contains sufficient fat to produce the required fluids.

43. SLOW COOKER PUERTO RICAN SHREDDED PORK

Prep Time:15 mins

Cook Time:8 hrs 10 mins

Additional Time:20 mins

Total Time:8 hrs 45 mins

Servings:6

Ingredients

- 1 tablespoon vegetable oil
- 1 (3 pound) boneless pork sirloin roast (trimmed and tied with kitchen twine, if necessary)
- 1 cup of orange juice
- 4 limes, juiced
- 4 cloves garlic, crushed and separated
- 1 tablespoon ground cumin
- 1 ½ tsp coarse salt
- 1 tsp dried oregano

Directions

1. In a sizable skillet, heat the oil over medium-high heat.

2. Make 3 to 5 holes in the pork roast with a sharp knife. Fill the holes with roughly half of the garlic. Cook roast for three minutes on every side in heated oil until completely browned. Place the roast in the slow cooker's crock.
3. Pour over the pork after blending the orange juice, lime juice, remaining garlic, cumin, salt, and oregano in a blender until smooth.
4. Turn the roast over and let the other side marinate for 10 minutes while the pork is allowed to sit in the orange juice mixture for 10 minutes.
5. Cook for 8 hours on Low in a slow cooker.
6. Onto a sliceting board, remove the pork. Use two forks to shred the meat.
7. Reserve 1 cup of the liquid after draining the slow cooker's crock. Pork shreds should be added back to the slow cooker crock, along with the conserved liquid.
8. Look on Low for 15 to 20 minutes, or until the meat is once more heated.

Cook's Tip:

- Ask your butcher to pre-tie the roast in the supermarket if you're not comfortable with the process.

44. PUERTO RICAN SOFRITO FROM SCRATCH RECIPE

Prep:10 mins

Active:15 mins

Total:10 mins

Serves:32 servings

Ingredients

- 2 medium Spanish onions, slice into large chunks (about 2 cups of)
- 4 cubanelle peppers, stemmed, seeded, and slice into large chunks (about 2 cups of)
- 1 large red bell pepper, cored, seeded, and roughly chop up (about 1 1/2 cups of)
- 4 ripe plum tomatoes, cored and slice into chunks (about 1 1/2 cups of)
- 1 large bunch cilantro, washed and roughly chop up (about 1 1/2 cups of)
- 18 medium cloves garlic, peel off

- 8 ajices dulces, stemmed (see note)
- 4 leaves of culantro (see note)
- Kosher salt

Directions

1. Put cubanelle peppers and onions in the workbowl of a food processor with a steel blade. Once coarsely chop up, pulse.
2. The other ingredients should be added through the feed tube one at a time while the motor is operating, and processed until smooth. Salt is used to flavor. Transfer to a container and freeze for later use or store in the refrigerator for up to three days.

Notes

- You can omit the dulces ajices if you can't locate them. If you can't get culantro, use more cilantro instead.

45. STUFFED TURKEY LEGS

Ingredients

- 2 turkey legs, boned (ask your butcher to do this if they don't already come this way)
- Olive oil, for frying
- For the stuffing
- 1 shallot, lightly chop up
- 20g butter
- 100g large field mushrooms, diced
- 2 rashers smoked streaky bacon, chop up
- 1 small free-range chicken breast, skin removed and chop up
- 1 medium free-range egg, beaten
- 70ml double cream
- 1 tbsp chop up fresh tarragon
- Handful spinach leaves, blanched and chop up

Method

1. In a sizable sauté pan set over medium heat, cook the shallot in the butter until it begins to turn golden. When the mushrooms have softened, add them. Add the bacon, season, and cook until browned. Set apart for cooling.
2. Purée the chicken after placing it in a food processor. Add 1 tbsp of egg and the cream, then blitz one more. Put the tarragon, spinach, and mushroom mixture in a bowl, mix it in, and season as need.
3. Lay the deboned turkey legs between sheets of cling film and flatten them slightly with a rolling pin. Make sure the skin completely encloses the flesh before adding the stuffing and reshaping it into a turkey leg. To fasten, tie with butcher's thread.
4. Set the oven's temperature to 190°C/fan 170°C/gas 5. The turkey should be cooked until golden brown on all sides in a hot, large frying pan with a generous amount of oil. Season and transfer to a rack in a roasting pan.
5. 1 14 hours of roasting. A leg is cooked if the juices run clear when a skewer is inserted into the middle of it. Serve with mashed potatoes, roasted parsnips, and Brussels sprouts.

46. SWEET PLANTAIN PIE RECIPE

PREP TIME 45 mins

COOK TIME 30 mins

INGREDIENTS

- 6 ripe plantains The riper they are the better. Not over ripe or soggy
- 1 box pie crust I used Pillsbury pie crust
- 1/4 cup of butter You'll need some to add a light coat in the piecrust, to grease pan and spread over the pie to bake.
- 3½ tbsp sugar If you're adding sugar to the crust, you'll need to set aside 1½ tablespoon sugar. If you're only going to add it to the pie, then you'll need 2 or adjust to your preference
- 2 tbsp cinnamon if you're using the cinnamon on the crust with the sugar, you'll use 1 tablespoon and the other for the sugar, butter cinnamon mix, to brush over the pie

INSTRUCTIONS

1. Peel the bananas
2. plantains diagonally split
3. 3 to 5 minutes of frying plantains
4. On a paper towel, drain the plantains.
5. Using a pizza sliceter or knife, slice the pie crust dough (about 312 inches broad).
6. Brush the dough lightly with some melted butter.
7. Since the sweet plantain may be very sweet, you may either opt to pour the sugar and cinnamon combination with butter over the entire pie or you can add some to the crust.
8. At the top of the pizza crust, add the slices, overlapping them and letting them hang over the crust just a little bit.
9. Over the plantains, fold the remaining half of the crust.
10. Plantain and the crust should be rolled together.
11. Put it in a pan or skillet and fill it all the way up.
12. In a saucepan, mix the remaining butter, sugar, and cinnamon.
13. Put a lot of melted butter on the cinnamon and sugar (leave a little for later)
14. 400° F for the preheating oven
15. Put pie in the oven.
16. For 30 minutes, bake
17. Take the pie out of the oven, then brush the remaining melted butter mixture on it.
18. Broil in the oven for a further three to five minutes.
19. Take out and eat warm with ice cream or plain

NOTES

- People with dietary limitations should consume as much sugar as they feel comfortable doing so. Keep in mind that some folks could prefer their desserts sweet when you're cooking for others.
- For this recipe, sweeter plantains work best.
- To prevent the plantain from burning and to let the crust brown a little more, tent wrap the pie with foil for a short period of time.
- Warm pie is preferable.
- Fun fact: This is a wonderful side dish or dessert for Thanksgiving.

47. TEA PARTY SANDWICHES (PUERTO RICAN VERSION)

Prep Time:30 mins

Total Time:30 mins

Servings:15

Yield:30 sandwiches

Ingredients

- 1 (12 ounce) can fully cooked luncheon meat (such as SPAM®), cubed
- 1 (16 ounce) jar processed cheese sauce (such as Cheez Whiz®)
- 1 (4 ounce) jar chop up pimiento peppers with liquid
- ¾ cup of mayonnaise-style sandwich spread with chop up sweet pickle
- 15 slices white bread
- 15 slices whole wheat bread
- 1 tsp dried parsley, or as need
- 1 small cucumber, thinly split

Directions

1. In a blender, mix the luncheon meat cubes, processed cheese sauce, pimientos, and sandwich spread. Blend until well mixd, stopping frequently to scrape down the sides of the blender. Put spread in a bowl.
2. 15 slices of white bread should have the mixture spread on them. Place a slice of whole wheat bread on top of every. Slice off crusts from sandwiches and lightly press them together. Sandwiches should be slice in half diagonally to form triangles. Parsley flakes should be sprinkled on sandwiches, and a slice of cucumber should be placed on top of every sandwich half.

48. TEMBLEQUE (PUERTO RICAN COCONUT PUDDING)

PREP TIME 10 mins

COOK TIME 10 mins

TOTAL TIME 20 mins

SERVINGS 8 servings

Ingredients

- 2/3 cup of granulated sugar
- 1/2 cup of cornstarch
- 1/4 tsp ground cinnamon
- Pinch salt
- 2 (13.5-ounce) cans full-fat coconut milk
- 1 1/2 tsp vanilla extract
- 1 (3-inch) peel of lime, non-compulsory
- 1 cinnamon stick, non-compulsory
- To garnish:
- 1/2 cup of sweetened coconut flakes, toasted
- 1 tsp ground cinnamon

Method

1. Dry ingredients should be whisked together in a sizable pot with a heavy bottom and preferably sloping sides. Mix the sugar, cornstarch, cinnamon powder, and salt. This is being done in a chilly, off-heat pot.
2. Add the coconut milk gradually:

3. Blend vanilla and one can of coconut milk with the sugar gradually. This will avoid any clumps in the sugar and cornstarch mixture and smooth it out. Add the remaining coconut milk and mix until a smooth, lump-free paste forms.

4. Add the lime and cinnamon stick: Add the cinnamon stick and lime peel.
5. Make the barbecue:
6. Set the saucepan on a medium heat source. While bringing the mixture to a simmer, whisk regularly. When tiny bubbles appear on the pan's edges, start whisking continuously but not aggressively. If you whisk too vigorously, too much air will be incorporated into the tembleque, which will result in bubbles in the final dessert that is molded.
7. In the end, simmer the tembleque on medium for 5–10 minutes, or until the whisk comes away from the pot with a ribbon attached.
8. Take the pot off the stove. While you rinse the mold, fish out and discard the lime peel and cinnamon stick from the tembleque (s).
9. Rinse the molds: Fill the mold with cold water and swirl it around to remove the soap, much like you would when cleaning dishes.
10. Fill your molds: Shake out any extra water, but don't let them dry. Utilizing a ladle or spoon, fill every mold. Spoon a cup of the heated liquid into every mold if you're using individual ones. Pour the entire custard into a 10-inch mold if you're serving dessert to a large group of people.
11. To release any air bubbles that may have become caught in the custard, gently tap the bottom of the mold against a countertop.
12. Refrigerate the tembleque until it is completely cooled. Press a sheet of plastic wrap firmly onto the tembleque's surface. Depending on the size of your molds, this could take two to four hours.
13. Carefully remove the custard from the mold and garnish: Use your fingertip or a thin, sharp knife to carefully pry the custard out from the mold. Allow gravity to release the custard from the mold by inverting it over a dish.
14. Serve the tembleque with ground cinnamon and toasted coconut flakes as garnish. The unmolded tembleque should be kept in the refrigerator in an airtight container or wrapped in plastic so that it touches the custard.

49. TEMBLEQUE DE COCO (COCONUT TEMBLEQUE)

Prep Time:15 mins

Cook Time:20 mins

Additional Time:4 hrs 40 mins

Total Time:5 hrs 15 mins

Servings:12

Yield:1 9-inch cake pan

Ingredients

- 4 cups of coconut milk
- 1 ½ cups of coconut cream
- 1 ½ cups of evaporated milk
- 1 tsp ground cinnamon
- ¼ tsp ground nutmeg
- ¼ tsp ground ginger
- 1 cup of milk
- 1 cup of cornstarch
- ⅔ cup of white sugar
- 1 ½ tsp vanilla extract
- 1 tsp orange blossom water
- ½ tsp salt
- ½ tsp lime zest
- 1 pinch ground cinnamon, or as need

Directions

1. In a sizable saucepan, mix the coconut milk, coconut cream, evaporated milk, cinnamon, nutmeg, and ginger.

2. Stir into the coconut milk mixture after combining the milk and cornstarch in a bowl and letting them dissolve. To the coconut milk mixture, add sugar, vanilla extract, orange blossom water, salt, and lime zest. Cook, stirring constantly, over medium heat until mixture is simmering and starting to thicken, about 5 minutes. Cook for about 15 minutes, reducing heat to medium-low, or until thickened.
3. After taking the saucepan off the heat, pour the mixture into a deep 9-inch cake pan and let it cool for about 30 minutes until room temperature. Wrap pan in plastic wrap and chill for at least 4 hours or overnight to ensure that the barbecue is cooled.
4. Take the barbecue out of the fridge and let it sit at room temperature for about 10 minutes. For one minute, submerge the pan's bottom in a bowl of warm water. By carefully running a tiny knife around the edges, carefully remove the tembleque from the pan. Invert the barbecue onto a serving plate that has been placed on top of the pan. Garnish with cinnamon.

Tips

The cake pan can be swapped out with an 8-cup of flavored gelatin mold ring or individual ramekins, if preferred.

50. TEMBLEQUE (PUERTO RICAN COCONUT PUDDING)

PREP TIME 5 minutes

COOK TIME 8 minutes

TOTAL TIME 13 minutes

Ingredients

- 1 13.5 ounces can coconut cream
- 1 13.5 ounces can coconut milk
- 1 cinnamon stick
- 1/2 to 3/4 cup of sugar
- 1/2 cup of cornstarch

- 1/8 tsp salt
- 1/4 tsp ground cinnamon (for topping)

Instructions

1. To pour the custard, have a 7-inch bowl (your pudding mold) available.
2. Mix salt, cornstarch, and sugar in a small bowl. Place aside.
3. Coconut cream, coconut milk, and a cinnamon stick should be simmered for 5 minutes in a large pan. Slice the cinnamon stick off.
4. The sugar mixture should be added all at once, and it should be thoroughly mixed in. 3 minutes of stirring is required. Pour the pudding into the mold bowl after turning off the heat. Give it one hour to rest at room temperature. Overnight or for two hours, chill.
5. The pudding in the bowl's edges should be slice with a knife. Carefully flip the bowl over by placing a plate over it. Without any issues, the pudding ought to slide onto the platter.
6. Add ground cinnamon to the pudding's surface. Slice, then dish.

Notes

- You can also use an 8x8 square baking dish.
- You may also spoon this pudding or custard into silicone muffin tins and serve it as separate treats.

51. PUERTO RICAN TOSTONES (FRIED PLANTAINS)

Prep Time:10 mins

Cook Time:10 mins

Total Time:20 mins

Servings:2

Ingredients

- 1 green plantain
- 5 tbsp oil for frying
- 3 cups of cold water
- salt as need

Directions

1. Slice the peel off plantain into 1-inch pieces. 3 cups of cold water should be put in a bowl.
2. Plantain slices are added in a uniform layer and fried until golden brown on both sides, about 3 1/2 minutes every side, in oil heated in a sizable deep skillet over medium-high heat. Put the skillet away.
3. Place the flattened slices of plantain on a sliceting board by flattening every one with a tiny plate. Place slices of plantain in cold water.
4. Slices of plantain should be cooked for one minute on every side in reheated oil in the skillet over medium heat. Serve right away after adding salt as need.

52. PUERTO RICAN CHRISTMAS COQUITO

Ingredients

- 100g of raisins
- 100ml dark rum
- 2 Tropical Sun Cinnamon Sticks
- 400ml Tropical Sun Sweetened Condensed Coconut Milk
- 400ml Tropical Sun Coconut Milk
- 100ml Tropical Sun Evaporated Coconut Milk
- 1/2 tsp Tropical Sun Nutmeg
- 1/2 tsp Tropical Sun Ground Cinnamon
- 1/2 tsp Tropical Sun Vanilla Extract

Method

1. Rum, raisins, and cinnamon should all be added to a pitcher and left to marinade for an hour.
2. Pour the other ingredients into the rum, raisin, and cinnamon mixture after blending them all in a blender.
3. At least 4 hours should pass before drinking. Have fun and celebrate!

53. VEGAN MOFONGO (FRIED MASHED PLANTAINS)

Prep Time:15 mins

Cook Time:30 mins

Total Time:45 mins

Servings:4

Yield:4 servings

Ingredients

- 5 large green plantains, coarsely chop up
- 1 (8 ounce) can organic tomato sauce
- 1 small bunch cilantro, chop up, or as need
- 2 tbsp homemade sofrito
- 2 tbsp olive oil, or as need, separated
- 1 clove garlic, chop up
- 1 (.18 ounce) packet sazon seasoning
- ½ cup of vegetable broth, or as need
- salt and ground black pepper as need

Directions

1. Plantains should be boiled for about 25 minutes with a pinch of salt in a 1-quart pot of water.
2. In a mortar or glass bowl, mash plantains with tomato sauce, cilantro, sofrito, 1 tablespoon olive oil, garlic, and sazon. Add the remaining 1 tablespoon of olive oil and just enough vegetable broth so that the mofongo holds together but is still dry enough to remove from a container with ease. Add salt and pepper as need.
3. Over the remaining 5 tbsp of vegetable broth, place the mofongo in a bowl and serve.

Cook's Note:

- Individual small mortars can also be used to mash the mofongo.

54. HOW TO PREPARE THIS RECIPE FOR CHIPOTLE CHICKEN IN THE AIR FRYER

INGREDIENTS

- 2 boneless, skinless chicken breasts, 6-8oz every
- 3 tbsp canned adobo sauce (see notes below)
- 2 tsp chipotle chile pepper powder
- 1 tablespoon brown sugar
- 1 tsp garlic powder
- 1 tsp onion powder
- ½ tsp dried oregano
- 2 tbsp olive oil
- Salt as need (about ½-1tsp)

INSTRUCTIONS

1. Mix the adobo sauce, chipotle chile powder, brown sugar, garlic powder, onion powder, oregano, oil, and salt in a shallow baking dish (see notes for a substitute). Mix thoroughly after mixing.
2. Add the chicken breast and coat with the mixture. Give it at least 30 minutes to marinate. (Overnight is preferable; four hours is better).
3. the air fryer for five minutes at 360 degrees Fahrenheit. Place the marinated chicken into the air fryer, and cook for 17 to 19 minutes (depending on size) at 360 degrees Fahrenheit, flipping once halfway through. When chicken is finished, the internal temperature should be 165 degrees F.
4. When the chicken is finished, remove it and let it five minutes to rest before eating.

5. Cooking Notes: Tobasco sauce The chipotles with adobo sauce will come in 7 ounce cans. For this dish, just use 3 tbsp of the sauce. Use 2 tbsp tomato paste, 1 tablespoon cider vinegar, 1 tsp cumin, and an additional tablespoon of olive oil as a replacement.

55. SHRIMP SOUP (SOPA DE CAMARONES)

Ingredients

- 4 tbsp butter or vegetable oil
- 30 medium shrimp about 1 pound peel off and deveined, tails on (heads and shells are non-compulsory)
- 1/2 cup of chop up onion
- 2 large garlic doves chop up
- 1/2 cup of chop up cilantro
- 1 cup of chop up tomato
- 1/2 cup of chop up green bell pepper
- 8 cups of water
- 1 tablespoon shrimp or chicken bouillon powder
- 1 tsp salt
- 1 cup of peel off and cubed potatoes 1-inch cubes
- 1 cup of split carrots 1/4-inch rounds
- 1/2 cup of heavy cream non-compulsory

Garnish:

- 6 lemon wedges

Instructions

1. Heat the butter or oil on high until it is piping hot in a large pot. Sauté all of the ingredients—shrimp, tomato, green bell pepper, onion, garlic, cilantro—for about a minute.

2. Bring to a boil after adding the water, salt, and bouillon powder. Add the potatoes and carrots, cover, and simmer for 10 to 15 minutes, or until the veggies are cooked, on medium heat.
3. If using, add the cream, mix, turn off the heat, and remove from stove. Correct the salt and serve the soup hot. Before eating, squeeze some lemon juice on top.

56. PUPUSAS DE QUESO (EL SALVADORAN CHEESE STUFFED TORTILLAS)

PREP TIME50 minutes

COOK TIME20 minutes

TOTAL TIME1 hour 10 minutes

Ingredients

For The Dough

- 2 c masa harina
- 1 ½ tsp salt
- 1 ½ - 1 ¾ c hot water
- For The Filling
- 1 c shredded jack cheese
- Oil for cooking

Instructions

1. In a bowl, mix salt and masa harina. Beginning with 1 1/2 cups of, pour in the hot water and stir until all of the masa is soaked and a light dough forms. (If extra water is required, add it.) Give it a covering and 15 minutes to stand.
2. To prevent the dough from sticking to your hands (and to help hydrate the dough if it crumbles as you form it, indicating it is too dry), dab your hands in some water. Pinch out a piece of dough the size of a golf ball (approximately 2 tbsp), then roll it

into a ball. With your thumbs, make a depression in the dough ball. In the hole, put roughly 2-3 tsp of cheese. To fill the hole and secure the filling inside the dough ball, pinch a little extra dough as necessary.
3. Repeat the process with the remaining dough, covering the masa balls that have been filled with a damp tea towel as you go.
4. Add a little oil to a skillet or griddle and preheat it to medium heat.
5. With your hands, flatten a full dough ball until it resembles a thick tortilla and measures about 3 inches in diameter. (Alternatively, you can flatten the tortillas using a tortilla press.)
6. Your shaped pupusa should be cooked for about 3 minutes per side on a hot griddle.
7. Repeat the process with the remaining pupusas, adding additional oil to the skillet as necessary to maintain a good, uniformly golden crust.
8. Serve hot on their own or alongside red salsa and/or curtido slaw.

Notes

- It is recommended to serve pupusas right away, while they are still hot and crispy. If you have any leftovers, reheat them in a toaster oven until crispy and thoroughly heated in a sealed container in the refrigerator.

57. CHICKEN IN WHITE WINE SAUCE

Prep Time 10 minutes

Cook Time 45 minutes

Total Time 55 minutes

Ingredients

- 12 cloves large garlic -smashed wt the side of a knife & peel off
- c ¼ extra virgin olive oil
- 2 lb ½ organic chicken thighss boneless/skinless
- 1 c white dry wine + an extra splash for the winos
- 1 c cherry tomatoes or grapes split in half
- 10 thyme sprigs or tarragon

- 1 bay leaf
- 1/4 c flat leaf Italian parsley roughly chop up
- 1 tsp sea salt + more as need
- black pepper as need freshly cracked
- 1 pinch sweet paprika

Instructions

1. Dry the chicken thoroughly on paper towels before liberally seasoning it with sea salt, black pepper, and a dash of paprika on both sides. Browning will be aided by the paprika.
2. A small amount of olive oil, just enough to thoroughly coat the bottom of a large cast iron pot, should be heated on a medium-low temperature. Make sure not to burn the garlic cloves as you add them to the pan and cook them on low heat until they are golden brown all over. Remove from the pan, reserve, and set aside.
3. Chicken chunks should be added to the hot oil skin-side down and seared until both sides are golden brown. (If necessary, work in batches, avoid overcrowding the pan, and add a little oil in between batches.)
4. While adding the wine and scraping out all the browned bits from the pan's bottom, remove and set aside the chicken. Garlic, thyme, and bay leaf should also be added back to the pan along with the chicken. Make sure you add enough wine to cover the chicken's sides by 34 of the way. After bringing to a simmer, let it reduce for five minutes.
5. For 45 minutes, or until the chicken is fork-tender and the white wine sauce has reduced to your preference, cover the pan tightly and cook it on low heat.
6. Toss the tomatoes with a generous amount of olive oil and sea salt in the meantime. For a few minutes in the broiler, until the tomatoes wilt and wonderful little charr marks appear on the top.
7. Place the broiled tomatoes on top of the chicken and serve with crusty bread or bruschetta, a good drizzle of extra virgin olive oil on top, and fresh parsley as a garnish.
8. Oven Approach!
9. Transfer the chicken to a 375°F oven after doing the aforementioned steps.
10. Cook for 45 minutes, or until the chicken is cooked through and the sauce is the consistency you choose. In the final 10 minutes of baking, top with tomatoes or grapes.

58. EL SALVADORAN ROAST TURKEY

PREP TIME:15 MINUTES

COOK TIME:5 HOURS

TOTAL TIME:5 HOURS 15 MINUTES

YIELD:6–12 SERVINGS 1X

ingredients

- 1 TURKEY, 12-20 POUNDS
- 1/2 CUP OF BUTTER, ROOM TEMPERATURE
- 1/4 CUP OF MUSTARD
- 1 CAN CAPERS, DRAINED
- 1 CAN GREEN OLIVES, DRAINED
- 64 OUNCES CHICKEN STOCK, OR MORE AS NEEDED
- 3 DRIED BAY LEAVES
- 1/2 CUP OF WHITE SESAME SEEDS
- 2 TABLESPOON PUMPKIN SEEDS
- 1 TBSP ANNATO SEEDS
- 2 TSP WHOLE PEPPERCORNS
- 1 28-OUNCE CAN OF STEWED, WHOLE TOMATOES
- 3/4 CUP OF WATER
- 3 GARLIC CLOVES, SMASHED
- 2 DRY CHILI PODS
- 1 TSP GROUND PAPRIKA
- 2 TSP SALT

instructions

1. Set the oven's temperature to 425.
2. With a paper towel, dry the defrosted turkey, then rub the butter and mustard into the skin. The dried bay leaves should be added to the bottom of the roaster with the

chicken stock. Place the turkey breast side up in the roaster without the rack and bake for 30 minutes.

3. Sesame seeds, pumpkin seeds, annato seeds, and peppercorns are lightly toasted in a small saucepan before being added to a blender container. Water, garlic, dried peppers, paprika, and salt should be added to the tomato liquid once it has been drained into the blender container. Blend the items until a paste forms. The remaining canned tomatoes should be added to the blender, then pulse until a salsa forms. Don't mix the capers and olives before adding them. More water could be required. Although thick, the salsa should be pourable.
4. Pour the blended tomato sauce over the entire turkey and reduce the oven temperature to 325 degrees after the turkey has cooked for 30 minutes. Re-bake the turkey in the oven, baste liberally every half an hour, and roast until the internal temperature reveryes 170 degrees. Normally, a turkey takes 15 minutes to cook every pound. As soon as the turkey begins to brown, cover it with foil. After resting, carve.
5. Place the carvings back into the salsa to marinate together if serving the meal traditionally (recommended). If extra stock is required to thin out, add it.
6. Alternately, slice the meat and serve it with the sauce as a side dish.

59. SALVADORIAN QUEZADILLA

PREP 15 min

COOK 50 min

INGREDIENTS

- 3 cups of granulated sugar
- 4 large eggs, separated1 can (12 fluid ounces)
- 2 cups of Cotija or grated parmesan cheese
- 3 cups of all-purpose flour, sifted
- 1 tablespoon baking powder
- 1 cup of (2 sticks) butter, melted
- 1 tablespoon sesame seeds

MAKE IT

1. Set the oven to 350° F. Use parchment paper to line a pan or baking dish that measures 13 x 9.

2. With an electric mixer set to medium speed, mix sugar, egg yolks, and 1/2 cup of evaporated milk in a large mixing bowl. Add cheese gradually and the remaining milk, scraping the bowl regularly.
3. Mix well after adding the flour, baking powder, and melted butter to the sugar mixture. In a medium mixing bowl, beat the egg whites until stiff peaks form. Mix batter and egg whites. Pour into the prepared baking dish. Add sesame seeds to the batter.
4. 50 to 55 minutes of baking time, or until a toothpick inserted in the center comes out clean. In pan, cool using a wire rack. Lift from pan and take paper out. Square them up.

60. TAMALES PISQUES

Prep Time1 hr 30 mins

Cook Time2 hrs

Total Time3 hrs 30 mins

Ingredients

For the dough

- 2 lb masa harina (nixtmalized maize flour)
- 2 tsp salt
- ½ cup of olive oil
- 1 onion , quartered
- 1 clove garlic
- 2 green bell peppers (bull's horn), seeded and diced
- 1 tablespoon vegetable bouillon powder (or chicken bouillon powder)
- 2 cups of water (more or less)

For the refried beans

- 2 lb red beans , cooked
- ½ cup of olive oil
- 1 onion , quartered

- 1 clove garlic
- 1 tomato , peel off, seeded, slice into 4
- ½ cup of boiling water
- Salt
- Pepper

For the tamales

- Banana leaves , slice into 30 squares of 10 inches (25 cm)
- Water
- Required material
- 30 (16-inch) square pieces parchment paper
- Cooking twine

Instructions

1. blended beans
2. Olive oil should be heated in a big Dutch oven at a medium temperature.
3. The tomato, onion, and garlic should be sautéed for five minutes with frequent stirring.
4. Add the red kidney beans, salt, and pepper, and cook for 10 minutes over medium-high heat while stirring frequently.
5. Put the oil and the rest of the preparation in a blender. When the mixture reveryes a thick but not overly solid consistency, add the hot water and mix. Add a little hot water if necessary. Place aside.
6. Tamale bread
7. In a skillet over medium heat, warm the oil.
8. Stirring often, sauté the green bell peppers, onion, and garlic for ten minutes.
9. Put the oil and the rest of the preparation in a blender.
10. Blend with 1/2 cup of water until a silky liquid is produced.
11. Add masa harina to the bowl of a stand mixer.
12. Salt and chicken bouillon powder should be added.
13. Add the previously mixd ingredients, then begin kneading.
14. Gently incorporate the remaining water while kneading to create a light dough (not solid).
15. If additional liquid or flour is required, stir until the desired consistency is reveryed.
16. a banana leaf
17. In a big pot, bring a lot of water to a boil.

18. Take one leaf at a time and, using a pair of pliers, submerge it for 5 seconds in boiling water.
19. Drain, then wipe yourself dry.
20. construction of the tamales
21. Put a banana leaf in the center of a piece of parchment paper.
22. Place about two tsp of dough in the center of the banana leaf, then press the dough down until it forms a circle.
23. 2 tsp of red bean purée should be positioned in the middle of the dough.
24. Close the tamale, giving it a rectangular or square shape, using the parchment paper. Use the cooking thread to bind the tamales.
25. Continue until all of the dough is consumed.
26. preparation of the tamales
27. The tamales should be put in a big Dutch oven.
28. Apply boiling water on top of them.
29. Cook for 1 hour and 30 minutes with the cover off.
30. During cooking, if necessary, add boiling water.

61. MOFONGO

Total: 40 min

Prep: 15 min

Cook: 25 min

Yield: 4 servings

Ingredients

- 4 green plantains
- Salt
- 4 cups of beef stock
- Oil, for frying
- 4 thick slices bacon
- 3 cloves garlic, chop up (1 tablespoon)
- Freshly ground black pepper
- Lime rinds, for serving
- Pork rinds, for serving

Directions

1. Slice plantains into 1-inch slices after peeling. A small amount of salt should be added to a medium dish of cold water. Plantain chunks should be soaked in water and then left aside.
2. Place a small saucepan over low heat, add the beef stock, and keep heated. A large skillet should have 1 inch of oil, which should be heated to 350 degrees F or just just smoking.
3. Cook bacon until crisp in a different pan or skillet; remove from pan and drain grease.
4. When the oil is ready, drain the chunks of plantain, pat them dry with paper towels, and then remove them from the water. Holding the plantain chunks against the side of the skillet and letting them slip into the oil can help you introduce them to the frying oil gently. Cook the plantains for about 5 minutes, or until golden brown.
5. Add the cooked plantains, bacon, garlic, salt, and pepper as need to the food processor while it is still hot. The ingredients should be processed until it resembles dough or mashed potatoes. If required, taste the mixture and adjust the seasoning. Quickly form the mixture into meatball-sized rough balls.
6. Put the plantains and warm broth in soup bowls. Serve the mofongo garnished with pork and lime rinds.

62. ACCRAS DE MORUE

Prep Time 25 minutes

Cook Time 30 minutes

Total Time 12 hours 55 minutes

Ingredients

- 1/2 pound salt cod
- 1 cup of parsley stems removed
- 3 scallions slice into 1" pieces
- 1/2-1 habanero pepper seeds and stems removed
- 3 cups of self rising flour
- 2 cups of water
- 1/2 tsp salt
- 1/2 tsp baking soda

Instructions

1. Put the codfish in a medium pot and add water to cover it. The water should be changed at least once while the fish is soaking in it for at least 12 hours or overnight. Remove the fish's water and then re-cover it with clean water. Bring the water and codfish to a boil in the pot on the burner. Cook for 15 minutes at a simmer after lowering the heat. Heat has been removed; set aside.
2. Parsley, scallions, and habaneros should all be placed in a small food processor. (A half pepper provides very little flavor and spice, whereas a full pepper adds more kick, which I appreciate!) Once the vegetables are lightly chop up, pulse several times. Place aside in a small basin after transfer.
3. Take the codfish out of the water. Break it up into big chunks using your hands. Fish should be added to the mini prep and pulsed until it is shredded lightly. Place aside.
4. Mix the flour and baking soda in a big bowl.

5. Salt should be dissolved in water. In the flour and baking soda mixture, make a well. Once you have a thick batter, gradually add the water. Mix well before adding the veggies and flakes cod.
6. Fryer or Dutch oven oil should be heated to 350–375 degrees. To pour out the batter, use a round tablespoon measure. Note: While working with hot oil, be gentle when scooping the batter into the oil. Don't drop it from a height of greater than 2-3 inches, or it will spill and probably hurt you. Instead, use the back of a spoon to gently scrape the batter into the oil. Your tester fritter is here. You should be able to determine from this one if the oil is exactly right or too hot, cold, or neither. The batter will sink to the bottom and take up to 10-15 seconds to float to the top if the water is too cold. Use a spider or slotted spoon to flip the marinade and brown on the opposite side after cooking for one or two minutes. Cook for a further minute or two until the outside is golden brown but the center is fully cooked. This is a tester, so you may evaluate your timing and oil, which may differ based on the machinery you're using.
7. Add 5 to 6 spoonfuls of batter to the oil and cook till browned once you've got the temperature and timing just right. Holding the spoon at an angle on the side of the fryer, scoop up marinades and drain the oil as much as you can. (Whether you can believe it or not, this truly removes a lot of the oil.) For a drying surface, move the marinades to a baking sheet lined with several layers of paper towels. Make marinades until all of the batter has been utilized.
8. Serve as a tasty hors d'oeuvre with beverages.

Nutrition

Calories: 68kcal | Carbs: 9g | Protein: 6g | Cholesterol: 11mg | Sodium: 590mg | Potassium: 137mg | Vit. A: 190IU | Vit. C: 3.4mg | Calcium: 18mg | Iron: 0.5mg

63. AFRICAN ADOBO-RUBBED TUNA STEAKS

Ingredients

For the avocado salsa:

- 2 ripe avocados, pitted, peel off, and slice into 1/2-inch cubes
- 3 scallions, white and green parts, thinly split on the bias
- 2 jarred piquillo peppers, diced (or substitute 2 jarred roasted red peppers)
- 2 cloves garlic, chop up
- 1/3 cup of fresh orange juice
- 1/4 cup of fresh lime juice
- 1/2 cup of extra virgin olive oil
- Kosher salt and freshly ground black pepper as need

For the adobo:

- 1 1/2 tsp toasted and ground coriander seeds
- 1 tsp ground ginger
- 1 1/2 tsp crushed red pepper flakes
- 1 1/2 tsp ground turmeric
- 1 1/2 tbsp dry mustard
- 1 1/2 tsp grated nutmeg
- 1 1/2 tsp ground allspice
- 1 1/2 tsp cayenne pepper
- 1 1/2 tsp freshly ground black pepper
- 1 1/2 tbsp kosher salt
- 1 tablespoon paprika
- 1 1/2 tbsp dried orange peel
- 1 tablespoon sugar
- Four 6-ounce tuna steaks
- 1/4 cup of peanut or canola oil

For the cucumbers:

- 2 1/2 tbsp sugar, or as need
- 1/2 cup of Champagne vinegar
- 1 European cucumber, peel off, halved lengthwise, seeded, and very thinly split

Instructions

1. The diced avocados, scallions, peppers, and garlic should all be mixd in a medium bowl. Mix the orange and lime juices with the salt, pepper, and olive oil in a separate bowl. Pour on top of the avocado mixture and stir gently. Allow to cool for 15 minutes.
2. For the cucumbers, in the meantime: The sugar and vinegar should be thoroughly mixd in a bowl. For about 15 minutes, add the cucumbers and let the mixture marinade.
3. Slice the cucumber neatly and place a slice on every plate before serving. Over the cucumbers, spread the tuna slices. Place a spoonful of the avocado salsa around or atop the tuna. Serve the cucumbers with a bit of the pickling liquids spooned around them. (Occasionally, I also garnish with a little grated orange zest.)
4. In a bowl, mix all the ingredients for the adobo.
5. Every of the tuna steaks should be thoroughly sprinkled with adobo and rubbed with 1 1/2 tsp of oil. (Save any leftover adobo spice rub for a different recipe.) The remaining 2 tbsp of oil should be heated in a nonstick skillet until it starts to smoke. The tuna is served rare and only needs a minute to sear on every side. Transfer to a plate, then reserve.
6. suggested wine: A surprising but pleasant addition would be a cold-pressed sake.
7. With Epicurious, chef Norman Van Aken offers the following advice:
8. There are Spanish piquillo peppers in the salsa. To use them, remove the peppers from the container, pat them dry, and then dice them. • The tuna can also be grilled, as long as there is adequate heat to immediately sear it. In a hurry, jarred roasted red peppers can be used. Put a lot of charcoal in a pyramid shape, let it burn until it turns white and is very hot, then spread it out into an even stack that is only a few inches away from the grate. Since you won't require a large cooking area, the coals don't need to cover the entire grill. Simply set the gas grill on high if using one. Cook the tuna for two to three minutes per side on an oiled grill rack after coating it with the oil and adobo as recommended.

64. ARROZ CON POLLO PERUANO

Prep15 MIN

Total60 MIN

Ingredientes

- 1 1/2taza de hojas de cilantro
- 4hojas de espinaca
- 4piernas y muslos de pollo, sin piel
- Sal y pimienta
- 1/4taza de aceite vegetal
- 1taza de cebolla picada fina
- 1cucharada de ajo picado
- 1/2taza de pasta de ají
- 1taza de cerveza
- 2tazas de caldo de pollo
- 1taza de aceite vegetal
- 2tazas de arroz de grano largo
- 1/4taza de alverjitas (petit pois, chícharos)
- 1/4taza de zanahoria cortada en cubitos
- 1/2pimiento rojo, cortado en
- 1taza de maíz blanco
- Salsa Criolla (ingredientes listados en paso 7)

Instrucciones

1. To make a homogeneous spaghetti, blend cilantro with the spinach and water in a food processor. Reserva.
2. Sazona sal y pimienta y seca el pollo con papel toalla. The oil is heated to a medium temperature in a bowl, and the chicken is fried until it is golden brown on all sides, about 7 minutes. Remove from the olla and place it on a plate.
3. Cebolla, oil, and aji amarillo pasta should all be heated in the same skillet for five minutes. Add the cilantro and chop up spinach and cook for three minutes. Add the beer, chicken broth, and chicken inside the olla.

4. Hierv, tap, and extinguish the fire. It simmers for 20 minutes. If necessary, adjust the seasoning by adding more salt and pepper.
5. 1 cup of oil is heated in another pan. Include the rice and thoroughly stir the dish. Add the alverjitas, zanahorias, pimiento, mazuela, and 3 1/2 tbsp. of the chicken stock you used to cook the chicken. Allow the stem to break, tap, lower the heat to the minimum, and let the food cook for 20 to 25 minutes. Revuelt with a tenedor and then tap again.
6. Serve the rice in four portions and top every with a chicken wing with Costa Rican Salsa when it's ready. If they would like a little bit of the juices used to cook the chicken as well.
7. Slice 1/2 of a red onion into very long, wide slices for the Salsa Criolla, lave well, and stir. Mixture with 1/2 a tomatillo thinly split, cilantro leaves, salt, pimiento, 1 lime juice, and 1 tablespoon of olive oil. Tijitas de aj can be added if desired.

65. BAKED BANANAS

Prep: 5 mins

Cook: 15 mins

Total: 20 mins

Ingredients

- 1 medium ripe banana slice in half lengthwise
- 1/2 tablespoon honey
- cinnamon as need

Instructions

1. Set the oven's temperature to 400F.
2. Place bananas on foil or a plate that can be baked.
3. sprinkled with honey and cinnamon.
4. Depending on how soft you prefer them, bake for 10 to 15 minutes with a foil cover tightly in place.

5. Enjoy as is or, at your discretion, serve with some whipped cream or light ice cream.
6. The next step is to rate and comment on the recipe to let us know how you liked it. This supports the success of our company and enables us to keep giving you free, excellent recipes.

Nutrition

Serving: 1 baked banana, Calories: 137 kcal, Carbs: 35.5 g, Protein: 1.5 g, Fat: 0.5 g, Sat fat: 0.2 g, Sodium: 2 mg, Fiber: 3 g, Sugar: 23 g

66. MEDITERRANEAN-STYLE WHOLE ROASTED RED SNAPPER

PREP – 10 MINS

COOK – 25 MINS

Ingredients

- 2 large whole snapper fish, cleaned and gutted
- 10 garlic cloves, chop up, and mixd with a pinch of salt
- 2 tsp ground cumin
- 2 tsp ground coriander
- salt
- 1 tsp black pepper
- 1 tsp ground sumac
- ½ cup of chop up fresh dill
- 3 bell peppers, different colors, split in rounds
- 1 large tomato, split into rounds
- 1 medium red onion, split into rounds
- Greek extra virgin olive oil, I used Private Reserve Greek EVOO

- 2 lemons

Instructions

1. Set the oven to 425 degrees Fahrenheit.
2. Dry the snapper by patting it. Create two slits on either side of the fish with a big knife. Every fish's intestinal cavity should be coated with the chop up garlic after being slit.
3. Put the cumin, coriander, salt, pepper, and sumac in a small bowl to prepare the spice mixture. To season the snapper on both sides, use 3/4 of the spice mixture; press the spices into the slits you previously made in the fish. For now, set the remaining 1/4 of the spice mixture aside.
4. Fill every intestinal cavity as full as you can with the chop up dill, peppers, tomatoes, and onions.
5. Put the stuffed fish on a baking sheet that has been lightly greased. The remaining split veggies should be added to create a border around the fish. Add a dash of salt and the remaining 1/4 of the spice mixture to the vegetables.
6. Olive oil should be liberally drizzled over everything.
7. Put the baking sheet on the bottom rack of an oven that has been preheated to 425 degrees F. Roast the fish for 25 minutes or until it flakes. Place the fish on a serving plate and top it with the juice of one lemon. Slice through the fish and portion it using the slits you previously made. Serve it with the remaining lemon wedges.
8. If you like, enjoy with a side of rice and a Fattoush salad.
9. Red snapper is marinated in strong Mediterranean tastes before being grilled to tenderness and served with colorful veggies.
10. 0 of the 4 minutes, 34 second time period
11. 90% volume

Notes

- Ask the fishmonger to butterfly the fish and clean it so it's ready to use to make things simple. If you'd like, you can request to have the head removed. But since it keeps the fish moist and improves flavor, I advise leaving the head on.
- The optimal time to prepare and roast a whole red snapper is just before you intend to consume it. However, you can slice the vegetables the night before and put them in separate airtight containers in the fridge to save some time.
- What to accompany: You scarcely need to add any sides to this sheet pan fish supper because it already has veggies. But there are some tasty alternatives, such Greek

potatoes or lemon rice. A dip like baba ganoush or tzatziki is always welcome. And a substantial salad is a requirement for me personally! Try the Fattoush, three bean salad, balela, or orange beet salad.
- The best way to consume this snapper dinner is right away. Keep any leftovers in the refrigerator for two to three days. Enjoy at room temperature, but if you must, reheat in an oven heated to 350 degrees F for no longer than necessary. Since fish tends to get overly dry when reheated, I'm not a big fan of doing it, however adding little water to your pan and covering the fish will help.
- For premium extra virgin olive oils and all-natural or organic seasonings, visit the Mediterranean Dish Shop. Make your own 3- or 6-pack of your preferred ingredients, such as the cumin, coriander, and sumac used in this dish!

Nutrition

Calories: 296.2kcalCarbs: 16.4gProtein: 95gFat: 7gSat fat: 1.4gPolyunSat fat: 2.3gMonounSat fat: 1.5gCholesterol: 166.5mgSodium: 300.9mgPotassium: 2292.6mgFiber: 4.5gSugar: 5.8g Vit. A: 2964.6IUVit. C: 121mgCalcium: 215.8mgIron: 2.9mg

67. BANANA SPLIT WITH CURRIED CHOCOLATE-COCONUT SAUCE

Ingredients

- 6 ounces bittersweet or semisweet chocolate, chop up
- 2 tbsp (1/4 stick) unsalted butter
- 1/4 cup of canned sweetened cream of coconut (such as Coco López)
- 2 tbsp dark rum
- 2 tsp curry powder
- 1 tsp lightly grated lime peel
- 3/4 cup of chilled whipping cream
- 1 tablespoon powdered sugar
- 4 bananas, peel off, halved lengthwise
- 1 quart vanilla ice cream
- 1 cup of 1/3- to 1/2-inch cubes peel off cored pineapple
- Sweetened flaked coconut, toasted

Instructions

1. Butter and chocolate are smoothed out in a medium saucepan over low heat. Add the next 4 ingredients and whisk. (Can be made one day in advance. Cover and let stand.) Over low heat, stir the sauce until it's just heated.
2. Cream and powdered sugar should be whisked to stiff peaks in a medium basin; chill until needed. Four long, shallow dishes should every contain two banana halves. Every dish should have 3 scoops of ice cream. Put heated sauce on top of the ice cream. Add whipped cream, pineapple, and toasted coconut on the top.

68. GARLIC MASHED YUCA ROOT

Prep Time: 10 mins

Cook Time: 30 mins

Total Time: 40 mins

Ingredients

- 1.5 lb yuca root, trimmed, peel off, and cubed
- 2 cloves garlic, smashed
- 1 tsp sea or kosher salt, + additional as need
- 2 c bone broth or water
- ½ tsp cracked black pepper
- 2 tbsp ghee, melted

Instructions

1. Using a sharp knife, trim the yuca root's ends before slicing it into three or four pieces across.
2. Place the slice side of every yuca piece up. Slice away the yuca's pink internal layer and waxy exterior brown skin, starting at the top and moving in a single, continuous motion. Continue by using the remaining pieces.
3. To get rid of any dirt or residue that may have migrated while trimming, rinse the peel off yuca root under cool running water before dicing the flesh into 1-inch pieces.
4. One tsp of salt should be added to the sauce pan along with the chop up yuca and crushed garlic. Cover the yuca with about an inch of water or broth. Heat the sauce pan on high until the water is boiling. Boil the yuca for about 20 minutes, reducing the heat to medium-high, or until the flesh can be easily mashed with a fork.
5. Return the yuca and garlic to the pot after draining the liquid. Alternately, add the yuca and garlic to a stand mixer's bowl.
6. To the pot or bowl, add the pepper and melted butter. Beat the yuca mash with a hand mixer or the paddle attachment on a stand mixer until it has a smooth consistency and a light, fluffy texture. Add more salt and pepper as need after seasoning as need. Serve hot. Yuca mash reheats well in the microwave and can be stored in the refrigerator for up to 3 days.

69. BUTTERNUT SQUASH WITH WALNUTS AND VANILLA

PREP TIME10 mins

COOK TIME30 mins

TOTAL TIME40 mins

SERVINGS4 servings

Ingredients

- 1 butternut quash, about 2 pounds, peel off, seeds removed, flesh slice into 1-inch cubes
- 3 bay leaves (if boiling the squash)

- 1 tablespoon extra virgin olive oil (if roasting the squash)
- Kosher salt
- 1 heaping cup of walnuts (can substitute pecans or pine nuts)
- 2 to 3 tbsp butter
- 2 tsp grated ginger
- 1 to 2 tsp vanilla extract
- Lemon juice
- 1/2 tsp dried thyme
- Freshly ground black pepper, as need

Method

1. Cubed squash can be roasted or boiled:
2. When roasting Set the oven to 400 °F. Spread out the cubed squash on a baking sheet and drizzle with a little olive oil. Add salt, toss, and roast for 20 minutes or until the cubes start to brown. Take out of the oven.
3. If boiling, add the bay leaves to a medium-sized pot with 4 cups of water. Simmer for a while. Squash can be added to the pot. Boil for 10 minutes with the lid on. Drain.
4. The walnuts are toasted:
5. The walnuts are toasted over medium-high heat in a sizable sauté pan. To prevent burning, stir them constantly. Remove from fire as soon as they begin to brown and emit the aroma of toasted walnuts.
6. Tips for Toasting Walnuts
7. MORE READING
8. Melt the butter: Place the pan of walnuts over medium-high heat and melt the butter. Add the squash after tossing the walnuts in the butter to coat them. Toss them in butter to coat.
9. Toss once more after adding the grated ginger, vanilla extract, black pepper, a little salt, and dried thyme. Squeeze some lemon juice over everything after turning off the heat. Add extra as need after tasting for salt and lemon.
10. Before serving, add another tablespoon or two of butter to make it a little more opulent.

70. CARIBBEAN CHICKEN KEBABS WITH LIME-CAYENNE BUTTER

Prep:12 mins

Cook:10 mins

Marinate:3 hrs

Total:3 hrs 22 mins

Ingredients

- ⅓ cup of orange juice
- ¼ cup of soy sauce
- 1 tsp chop up fresh ginger
- 2 garlic cloves, chop up
- 2 pounds boneless, skinless chicken breasts, slice into 1 1/2-inch pieces
- 1 sweet onion, slice into 1 1/2-inch pieces
- 2 orange or red bell peppers, slice into 1 1/2-inch pieces
- 1 pineapple, cubed
- 1 pint cherry or grape tomatoes
- Lime-Cayenne Butter

Directions

1. In a wide zip-top bag or shallow dish, mix the first 4 ingredients. Stir in the chicken and onion after adding them. For 3 to 6 hours, refrigerate.

2. Drain the chicken and onion; throw away the marinade. On 10 or 12 (10-inch) skewers, thread the chicken, onion, and following three ingredients. Use Lime-Cayenne Butter to scrub.
3. Grill the chicken for 8 to 10 minutes, turning it over and baste it frequently with lime-cayenne butter over medium heat (325 to 350°).

71. CARIBBEAN COCONUT CURRY SAUCE

Ready In: 50mins

INGREDIENTS

- 2/3cup of canned cream of coconut (such as Coco Lopez)
- 1/2cup of fresh lime juice
- 6tbsp chop up green onions
- 2tsp curry powder
- 1/2tsp cayenne pepper
- 1/2tsp salt

DIRECTIONS

1. Coconut cream and lime juice are smoothed together in a small bowl.
2. Salt, cayenne pepper, green onions, and curry powder should be stirred in.
3. (Can be made one day in advance. Cover and put in the fridge.) Before and during grilling, brush the chicken or shellfish with half of the sauce.
4. Separately serve the remaining sauce.

NOTE:

- I usually serve this dish with a side of frijoles negros (black beans) and saffron rice cooked with pineapple juice instead of water.

72. CARIBBEAN PUMPKIN AND BLACK BEAN SOUP

PREP TIME 10 Min

COOK TIME 30 Min

METHOD Stove Top

Ingredients

- 15-oz can with 1 tsp ground cumin
- purely pureed pumpkin
- 1 can of drained 15-ounce black beans 1 can of light, unsweetened coconut milk
- Canned vegetable broth, 1 cup of
- Fresh lime juice and four tbsp of chop up fresh cilantro
- Grated lime peel, 3/4 tsp.

DIRECTIONS

1. How to Prepare Caribbean Black Bean and Pumpkin Soup
2. 1 Stir the cumin for 30 seconds in a heavy medium saucepan set over medium heat. Add 3 tbsp of cilantro along with the pumpkin, beans, coconut milk, and broth.
3. I suggest justapinch.com Recipes & Searches
4. Stirring continuously, bring soup to a boil. To integrate flavors, lower heat to medium-low and simmer for at least 3 minutes.
5. Lime peel and juice should be mixd. Use salt and pepper to season the soup.
6. Put the soup in bowls. Add the final tablespoon of cilantro.

73. CARIBBEAN RICE AND BLACK BEAN SALAD

Ready In: 10mins

INGREDIENTS

- 1/2cup of olive oil
- 1/4cup of cider vinegar
- 1tablespoon Dijon mustard
- 1tsp cumin
- 1tsp chop up garlic (no more than 1 tsp or less of fresh garlic, as it will be too overpowering!)
- 1tsp sugar (non-compulsory)
- salt and black pepper (as need)
- cayenne pepper (non-compulsory)
- 2 1/2cups of cooked long-grain rice (room temperature or cold, about 1 cup of uncooked)
- 1(15 ounce) can black beans, rinsed and well drained
- 1(10 ounce) can canned corn niblets, well drained
- 1small yellow bell pepper, seeded and chop up
- 1small red bell pepper, seeded and chop up
- 3green onions, chop up (can use more or less)

DIRECTIONS

1. Mix the oil, vinegar, Dijon mustard, cumin, and garlic in a small bowl until well mixd. Add salt and pepper as need and, if you think the dressing is too powerful, additional sugar.
2. Mix the cooked rice, black beans, corn niblets, bell peppers, and green onions in a medium bowl.
3. You only need to add a small quantity of dressing to moisten and mix the ingredients.
4. Refresh the seasoning with salt and pepper (or cayenne pepper).
5. Can be prepared in advance; cover and chill.

74. CHICKEN AND PORK STEW WITH PLANTAINS AND POTATOES

Ingredients

- 3 green bananas, 1
- Extra-virgin olive oil, 1/4 cup of
- 4 smashed garlic cloves
- 1/4 cup of dried oregano
- two salty tsp
- Cayenne pepper, 12 tsp
- 12 tsp of allspice, ground
- 1 1/2 pounds of 1 1/2-inch cubes of skinless, boneless chicken thighs
- 1 1/2 pounds of boneless, 1 1/2-inch cubed pork spareribs or pork butt
- 2 cups of chicken broth low in salt
- Tomato dice in juice, 1 15-ounce can
- 1 big onion, diced into half-inch pieces
- 1/2-inch-sized chunks of 1 fairly large green pepper
- apple cider vinegar, 3 tsp
- Red potatoes: 1 pound, cleaned, and diced into 1 1/2-inch pieces
- 2 ears of corn, split into rounds 1 1/2 inches thick.
- Chop up fresh cilantro, 12 cup of

Preparation

1. Trim the ends off the plantains and slice their skin four times vertically (do not slice into fruit). Pull off the peel after one minute at 50% power in the microwave.
2. In a large pot, stir the following six ingredients until a paste forms. Mix meats. Cook meats for about 10 minutes, stirring frequently, over high heat until the outsides are no longer pink. Vinegar, plantains, juiced tomatoes, onions, peppers, and vinegar should be added. heating to a boil Medium-low heat should be used; cover and simmer for 20 minutes. Add corn and potatoes to the pot. For 40 minutes, simmer covered. Add salt and pepper as need. Adding cilantro last.

75. CHILI-RUBBED SALMON WITH AVOCADO SALSA

Prep Time:5 mins

Cook Time:15 mins

Total Time:20 mins

Ingredients

Chili-Rubbed Salmon

- 4 salmon fillets (5-6 oz portions)
- 2 tbsp olive oil
- 3 tbsp brown sugar (packed)
- 1.5 tbsp chili powder
- 1 tsp ground cumin
- 1 tsp black pepper
- 1 tsp salt

Avocado Salsa

- 2 avocados (diced into ½ inch cubes)
- 4 tbsp cilantro leaves (torn or chop up)

- ½ cup of cherry tomatoes (quartered)
- 1 lime (juiced)
- salt + pepper (as need)

Instructions

1. Guacamole Salsa
2. Mix the avocados, cilantro, cherry tomatoes, and lime juice in a bowl. Add salt and pepper as need.
3. Salmon with a Chili Rub
4. Grill should be warmed to a medium heat (425–450°F).
5. Mix brown sugar, chili powder, ground cumin, pepper, and salt in a small bowl.
6. Olive oil should be sparingly brushed on salmon fillets.
7. The salmon fillets should be liberally covered in the rub.
8. Place the salmon on the grill skin side down after thoroughly greasing it. Cook the fish for 4 minutes with the lid on. Place the lid back on the grill, turn the salmon over carefully, and cook it for an additional 4 minutes.
9. Once the salmon has been cooked to an internal temperature of 125°F, transfer it to a plate that has been cleaned, cover it with a baking dish, and bake it for 5 minutes.
10. Serve the salmon with the avocado salsa spooned on top.
11. a Bake
12. Oven: Preheat to 425 °F.
13. Salmon should be baked for 10 to 12 minutes, or until it reveryes an internal temperature of 125°F, on a baking sheet lined with parchment paper.
14. After transferring, place a baking dish on top and wait five minutes.

Tips:

Meal + Storage Salmon can be stored after cooking for up to 4 days, but it is generally best eaten right away. Brown sugar does not remain in fresh avocado salsa. You may prepare the chili rub in advance and keep it in the cabinet for up to a year.

Nutrition Information

Serving: 1/4 batch, Calories: 432kcal, Carbs: 20g, Protein: 25g, Fat: 29g, Sat fat: 4g, Cholesterol: 62mg, Sodium: 693mg, Potassium: 1163mg, Fiber: 8g, Sugar: 10g, Vit. A: 1200IU, Vit. C: 14.3mg, Calcium: 48mg, Iron: 2.6mg

76. CHOCOLATE-ANISE STRAWS

Active Time 20 minutes

Total Time 1 hour

Ingredients

- 1 tsp anise seeds
- 1 1/2 ounces fine-quality bittersweet chocolate (not unsweetened), chop up
- 2 1/2 tbsp sugar
- 3 (17- by 12-inch) phyllo sheets
- 3 tbsp unsalted butter, melted

Instructions

1. Turn on the 375°F oven.
2. An electric coffee/spice grinder or a mortar and pestle can be used to lightly grind anise. Use a food processor to lightly chop sugar, anise, and chocolate.
3. To create six sheets, slice the phyllo sheets in half crosswise. Cover with two plastic wrap sheets that cover every other and a moist kitchen towel after that. Place 1 phyllo sheet on a work surface, long side facing you (keep other sheets covered), and lightly brush lower half of sheet with butter. Place a heaping tablespoon of the chocolate mixture in the center of the baking sheet, lengthwise. Enclosing the chocolate with a folded phyllo sheet, lightly brush with butter. Roll the dough firmly

to create a 12-inch straw, beginning with the chocolate-facing side. Transfer five more straws in the same way, seam side down, to a baking sheet.
4. Straws should be baked for 12 to 14 minutes in the upper third of the oven, until brown. Let them cool on a rack. To create 12 straws, slice every in half.

Note

- from the chef: Straws last two days in an airtight container.

77. CHOCOLATE CINNAMON RICE PUDDING

yield: 6 - 8

prep time: 5 MINUTES

cook time: 40 MINUTES

total time: 45 MINUTES

Ingredients

- 2 cups of Milk (2% works well)
- 1/2 cup of Jasmine or Basmati uncooked rice, I used Jasmine (can use a short-grain rice, Arborio, if preferred)
- 1 tsp Vanilla extract
- 1/2 tsp ground Cinnamon
- 1/4 tsp Salt
- 2 Tbls unsweetened Cocoa Powder, I prefer the dark cocoa variety
- 1/2 cup of Sugar
- Slivered Almonds, toasted for garnish (non-compulsory)

Instructions

1. All the ingredients—aside from the roasted almonds—should be mixd in a medium saucepan over medium-high heat. Stir well to mix.
2. Gently bring to a boil. Simmer (uncovered) for 30 to 40 minutes over low heat, stirring occasionally to keep mixture from sticking to the bottom of the pan.
3. Serve warm or cold and, if preferred, top with toasted, slivered almonds.
4. To stop a skin from forming when storing, cover with plastic wrap that touches the service.
5. will last up to 3 days if covered and kept in the fridge.

78. DAIQUIRI

Ingredients

- 2 ounces light rum
- 1 ounce lime juice, freshly squeezed
- 3/4 ounce demerara sugar syrup
- Garnish: lime twist

Instructions

1. In a shaker with ice, mix the rum, lime juice, and demerara sugar syrup. Shake vigorously until thoroughly cold.
2. Into a chilled coupe, strain.
3. Add a lime twist as garnish.

79. CLASSIC HAVANA FRITTATA

Ingredients

- 1 large ripe plantain, slice into 1/2-inch cubes
- 1 medium baking potato, peel off and slice into 1/2-inch cubes
- Canola oil
- 8 large eggs
- 1/2 cup of heavy cream
- 1 tsp sweet paprika
- Salt and pepper as need
- 3 tbsp olive oil
- 2 tbsp butter
- 1 large yellow onion, diced

Instructions

1. Fry the potato and plantain separately in the canola oil until they are crisp-tender.
2. Whisk the heavy cream, eggs, and paprika in a large bowl. Season with salt and pepper.

3. Over medium-high heat, add the butter and olive oil to a 10-inch sauté pan with an ovenproof handle. The onion is added when the butter has melted, and it is sautéed until brown.
4. Stir in the potato and plantain before pouring the egg mixture into the pan. Cook for 5 minutes, periodically scraping the pan to ensure the bottom settles.
5. Place under the broiler for 7 to 10 minutes, or until golden brown. Serve alongside a basic mesclun salad (non-compulsory).

80. HOW TO MAKE TRINIDAD COCONUT BAKE

Prep Time: 10 minutes

Cook Time: 20 minutes

Proofing time: 40 minutes

Total Time: 1 hour 10 minutes

Ingredients

1. 4 cups of flour all-purpose, bread flour, or a 50:50 combination
2. 2 cups of coconut milk
3. 1 cup of shredded coconut
4. 1/4 cup of softened butter unsalted or salted, if preferred
5. 2 tsp yeast
6. 1 tablespoon sugar brown, coconut, white, etc.
7. 1/4 tsp salt
8. 1/4 tsp ground nutmeg powder

Instructions

1. The flour, yeast, sugar, salt, and spice should all be mixd in a big bowl.
2. Mix the flour with the butter after adding it. Making the mixture crumbly with my hands is my preferred method because it makes the dough simpler to handle.
3. Coconut milk and coconut shreds should be added.
4. Note: I typically reheat milk until it is lukewarm. When you pour a few drops on your wrist, it should feel comfortable, but you don't want to heat it up too much. The yeast will be activated by doing this.
5. To thoroughly include all the ingredients, knead the dough for a few minutes.
6. Fill a bowl with the dough and lightly oil it. Then cover it and leave it for 20 to 25 minutes to rest before baking. It will expand by double.
7. Butter a baking dish or a typical baking tray liberally.
8. Press the dough firmly into the baking dish to remove all the air.
9. Spread it out as you apply pressure, making the extremities somewhat thinner than the center.
10. Make holes in the dough's surface all over using a fork. After that, give it another 15 to 25 minutes to relax.
11. The oven should be preheated to 400°F/200°C in the interim.
12. The bread should be baked for around 20 minutes, or until it turns a pale golden color. Before slicing it, let it cool fully.
13. How to Keep
14. The coconut bake should be consumed within two days, although it can be stored in the refrigerator for up to four days. After it has totally cooled, make sure to wrap it tightly. I enjoy toasting or reheating leftovers!
15. Wrap the bread carefully after letting it cool completely (you could also do this with individual pieces, instead). You can freeze it for three to five months. Just place it in the refrigerator to thaw (the loaf will probably need to thaw overnight and individual pieces would take a couple of hours).

Notes

- Elective add-ons:
- You are welcome to add your own additions and adjustments to this coconut bake in order to make it even more delicious. Here are some suggestions:
- Use vegan butter or margarine to make it vegan.
- To provide a lovely texture, mix in some chop up almonds, raisins, and carrot shreds.

- Alternatively, you could spice it up even more by including ginger, cinnamon, or anise!
- Served with a number of foods, including salted fish dishes like Salted Cod Salad, this coconut bake recipe is also delicious with cheese, butter, or jam. When it it comes out of the oven, I personally adore it with butter! Sandwiches made with this coconut bake would be fantastic!
- For more advice and solutions to frequently asked questions, read the blog post!

Nutrition

Calories: 368kcal | Carbs: 58g | Protein: 8g | Fat: 12g | Sat fat: 8g | PolyunSat fat: 1g | MonounSat fat: 2g | Trans Fat: 1g | Cholesterol: 15mg | Sodium: 156mg | Potassium: 136mg | Fiber: 3g | Sugar: 8g | Vit. A: 177IU | Vit. C: 1mg | Calcium: 38mg | Iron: 3mg

81. COCONUT FLAN RECIPE

Prep Time 15 minutes

Cook Time 45 minutes

Total Time 1 hour

Ingredients

- 1 cup of sugar
- ½ cup of water and if possible, a few drops of lemon/lime juice to avoid crystallization
- 14 oz sweetened condensed milk
- 14 oz canned coconut milk
- 5 eggs at room temperature
- 1 tsp pure vanilla extract

Instructions

1. Oven should be heated to 350° F (180° C).
2. Stir together sugar, water, and a few drops of lemon juice in a nonstick medium skillet or saucepan. Cook over medium heat until the sugar is dissolved and has taken on an amber hue (about 8-10 minutes). Be careful not to stir or otherwise muck with the mixture as it cooks! Pour the caramel into an 8-inch round pan, immediately swirl it to coat the bottom and edges, and then leave it to solidify for at least 3 to 5 minutes.
3. Blend the sweetened condensed milk, coconut milk, eggs, and vanilla for 30 to 60 seconds, or until the mixture is smooth and the eggs are completely gone. Fill the pan with the mixture.
4. By setting the flan pan inside a 13x9-inch baking pan, you may start the bain-marie (water bath). Boiling water should revery halfway up the flan pan in the outer pan.
5. Bake the coconut flan for 45 minutes, or until it is set but still somewhat jiggly. For around 30 minutes, move the flan pan to a wire rack. After that, put the flan in the refrigerator for at least 4 hours, or until it is cold.
6. To remove the mold, gently run a paring knife over the pan's edges after warming the bottom of the pan on a warm water bath for about 3 to 5 minutes. To unmold the flan, place a big plate over the pan and flip it while tightly holding onto it.
7. Flakes of coconut can be used as a garnish. up until serving time, chill!

Cookbook Notes

- The coconut flan can be kept in the refrigerator for up to 5–6 days when sealed in a container. Don't freeze it since when it thaws, the smooth texture will change.

Nutrition

Calories: 274kcal | Carbs: 37g | Protein: 6g | Fat: 13g | Sat fat: 9g | Cholesterol: 79mg | Sodium: 74mg | Potassium: 236mg | Fiber: 1g | Sugar: 36g | Vit. A: 187IU | Vit. C: 2mg | Calcium: 110mg | Iron: 1mg

82. COCONUT RICE AND PEAS

Ingredients

- 1 cup of soaked and drained dried red kidney beans

- butter, unsalted, in tbsp
- 1 big shallot, chop up lightly
- 1 tablespoon of oregano, chop up
- 1 tsp of thyme, chop up
- 2 grated, lightly chop up garlic cloves
- salt kosher, pepper freshly ground
- Unsweetened coconut milk in a single 13.5-ounce can
- a serving of basmati rice

Preparation

1. In a large saucepan, the beans should be covered with 6 cups of cool water. Bring to a simmer over medium heat, skimming off froth as necessary, and then reduce heat to maintain a barely simmering condition. Beans should be cooked for one to twelve hours with water added as needed to maintain them at least one inch covered.
2. Melt the butter in a medium skillet over medium heat. At this time, add the shallot, oregano, and thyme. Cook for approximately 4 minutes, stirring often. The garlic should be added and stir-fried for about a minute, or until fragrant. From the stove, remove the skillet. With a slotted spoon, add the beans to the skillet and stir to mix. As need, add salt and pepper. Set aside.
3. To the remaining 2 cups of the bean boiling liquid, add the coconut milk, and then reduce the heat to a simmer. While the liquid is cooking, the rice should be put in a fine-mesh strainer and washed in cold water until the water is clear. Add the rice, turn the heat down to a simmer, and then cover the pan. After the rice has cooked for ten minutes, uncover it and stir in the bean mixture you've stored. After tasting the dish, add salt if necessary. Till the rice is tender, cook it in a covered pan for 8 to 10 minutes. Remove from heat and then cover. the rice with a fork.
4. One hour in advance, you can make the rice and beans. Keep your cover. Slowly reheat before serving.

Nutrition Per Serving

Calories (kcal) 260

Fat (g) 4.5

Sat fat (g) 3

Cholesterol (mg) 10

Carbs (g) 47

Dietary Fiber (g) 4

Total Sugars (g) 0

Protein (g) 7

Sodium (mg) 30

83. COCONUT SHRIMP WITH TAMARIND GINGER SAUCE

Ready In:1hr 30mins

INGREDIENTS

FOR SAUCE

- 1tsp tamarind paste
- 1 1/2tbsp fresh lime juice
- 2/3cup of mayonnaise
- 1 1/2tbsp mild honey
- 2tsp Dijon mustard
- 1tsp lightly grated peel off fresh ginger
- 1/4tsp salt

FOR SHRIMP

- 4cups of sweetened flaked coconut (10 ounces)
- 1cup of all-purpose flour

- 3/4cup of beer (not dark)
- 3/4tsp baking soda
- 1/2tsp salt
- 1tsp cayenne
- 1large egg
- 6cups of vegetable oil
- 48medium shrimp, peel off, leaving tail and first segment of shell intact, and, if desired, deveined (1 1/2 pound)

DIRECTIONS

1. Create sauce:
2. In a small bowl, stir lime juice and tamarind concentrate until mixd. Add the last few sauce ingredients and mix well. Cover and chill.
3. Shrimp preparation:
4. Chop coconut coarsely, then add half to a pie plate or shallow soup bowl.
5. In a small bowl, stir together the egg, flour, beer, baking soda, salt, and cayenne.
6. Oil should be heated to 350°F on a thermometer in a 4- to 6-quart deep heavy pot over fairly high heat.
7. shrimp with coating while oil is heating.
8. Holding one shrimp by the tail, dip it into the batter, letting the excess drop off, and then coat it entirely in the coconut, pushing gently to help it stick. Transfer to a dish and repeat with the remaining shrimp, adding more coconut to the bowl as necessary.
9. Batches of 8 shrimp should be fried in the oil for about a minute, rotating once, until golden. With a slotted spoon, transfer to paper towels to drain and lightly salt. Between batches, remove any coconut from the oil and reheat it to 350°F.
10. Serve sauce with the shrimp.

84. COFFEE-BEAN GRANITA

INGREDIENTS

- 4 cups of water

- 1 cup of sugar
- 2 1/2 cups of whole coffee beans (about 6 ounces)
- 1/4 cup of coffee liqueur (such as Tia Maria or Kahlua)

DIRECTIONS

1. In a large saucepan, mix sugar and 4 cups of water. Bring to a boil while stirring to dissolve the sugar. 3 minute boil. Add coffee beans and simmer for 2 minutes. Remove pan from heat; cover and soak for about 3 hours, or until mixture is cool.
2. Coffee beans in the strainer should be discarded before pouring the liquid into a 13x9x2-inch glass baking dish. Stir in coffee liqueur to the liquid in the dish.
3. Stirring every 45 minutes, freeze until firm, takes around 5 hours. (Can be made three days in advance. Keep refrigerate and covered.)
4. Use a fork to scratch the granita's surface until crystals form before serving. Granita should be removed and served with an ice cream scoop. about 8 servings total. Contrary to what I would have expected, the flavor of boiled beans is actually rather vibrant and aromatic without being overpowering. Alcohol adds color and a pleasant flavor boost while also preventing the mixture from freezing solid. Even though brewed coffee will certainly work just as well, the flavor might be too overpowering.

85. CRAB AND CHORIZO FRITTERS

Ingredients

- 1 cup of water
- 1/2 cup of (1 stick) butter
- 1 1/4 tsp salt
- 1 cup of all purpose flour
- 1 tsp ground cumin
- 4 large eggs
- 1/2 cup of lightly chop up dry-cured link chorizo (about 2.2 ounces)
- 2 tbsp sofrito*
- 1/2 pound lump crabmeat

- Canola oil (for frying)

DIRECTIONS

1. Stirring constantly, bring 1 cup of water, butter, and salt to a boil in a heavy medium pot. Add cumin and flour. 3 minutes of vigorous stirring. Get rid of the heat. After every addition, thoroughly incorporate in the eggs one at a time. Add chorizo and sofrito, chop up. Add crabmeat and stir slowly.
2. Fill a heavy, big saucepan with enough oil to cover the bottom by 3 inches. Heat to 375°F over medium heat. Working in batches, carefully drop tablespoonfuls of dough into the oil, smoothing slightly with the back of a metal spatula. Fry the fritters for about five minutes total, turning them once so that all sides are cooked through and browned.
3. Serve fritters after transferring them to paper towels to dry.

86. CRAB AND COCONUT DIP WITH PLANTAIN CHIPS

Active time: 20 min

Start to finish: 20 min

Ingredients

- 1/3 cup of well-stirred unsweetened canned coconut milk
- 3 scallions, chop up
- 1 tsp chop up fresh jalapeño chile, including seeds
- 1/2 cup of chop up fresh cilantro
- 1/2 cup of mayonnaise
- 3 tbsp fresh lime juice, or as need
- 1 lb jumbo lump crab meat, picked over and coarsely shredded

DIRECTIONS

1. Pour into a bowl after thoroughly blending coconut milk, scallions, jalapenos, and 1/4 cup of cilantro in a blender. Juice, mayonnaise, and the final 1/4 cup of cilantro should all be blended justly. Serve with spoons on top of plantain chips after adding crab and salt as need.
2. Your recipes from Epicurious & Bon Appétit have come to an end. Now subscribe. Sign In if you're already a subscriber.

Chef's note:

- Prepare the dip six hours in advance, cover it, and refrigerate. Before serving, stir.

87. CREAM CHEESE FLAN

Prep Time: 10 mins

Cook Time: 1 hr

Chill: 2 hrs

Total Time: 1 hr 10 mins

Ingredients

- 1/2 cup of sugar
- 1 package (8 ounces) cream cheese, softened
- 5 eggs
- 1 can (12 ounces) evaporated milk

- 1 can (14 ounces) condensed milk

Instructions

1. When the sugar is caramelized and yellow, put it in a skillet and simmer it slowly. To keep the sugar from burning and to evenly distribute the melted liquid on the mold's bottom, move the pan back and forth over the flames many times.
2. After taking it off the heat, immediately pour the caramel into an 8-inch circular pan and swirl it to coat the bottom with a thin layer of caramel.
3. Cream cheese should be lightly beaten in a big bowl using an electric mixer. till frothy and smooth.
4. One at a time, beat after every addition of an egg.
5. Stir in the condensed milk and evaporated milk until thoroughly mixed. To allow part of the foam to subside, let the mixture sit for a while. A different option is to blend the eggs, evaporated milk, condensed milk, and cream cheese together.
6. Put the mixture in the round pan that has been prepared.
7. Place llaneras in a broad, oven-safe dish with about 1 inch of water, covered with foil (water bath).
8. 50 to 1 hour of baking time at 375 degrees Fahrenheit, or until a toothpick inserted in the center of the custard comes out clean.
9. Remove from the oven, let cool, and then place in the refrigerator to set. Turn the flan over onto a serving platter to serve, finishing with a layer of caramel.

Notes

1. You can alternatively cook the flan in ramekins called llaneras, which hold about four every.
2. For stovetop cooking, steam the food for 30 to 40 minutes over medium heat, or until a toothpick inserted in the center comes out clean.

Nutrition Information

Calories: 267kcal, Carbs: 29g, Protein: 8g, Fat: 13g, Sat fat: 7g, Cholesterol: 108mg, Sodium: 159mg, Potassium: 263mg, Sugar: 29g, Vit. A: 510IU, Vit. C: 1.4mg, Calcium: 199mg, Iron: 0.5mg

88. CURRY-COCONUT MUSSELS

Ready In: 1hr

INGREDIENTS

- 1/2 medium onion, lightly chop up
- 2 garlic cloves, chop up
- 1 tablespoon lightly grated peel off fresh ginger
- 2 tbsp vegetable oil
- 1/2 cup of dry white wine
- 1/2 cup of fresh orange juice
- 1/4 cup of fresh lime juice
- 1 tsp curry powder
- 1 tsp chop up fresh thyme
- 3/4 tsp lightly crumbled saffron thread
- 1 bay leaf (not California)
- 1 (14 ounce) can unsweetened coconut milk
- 1 tomatoes, peel off, seeded, and chop up
- 1/2 tablespoon sambal oelek (chile paste)
- 2 tbsp chop up fresh cilantro
- 2 lbs mussels, well scrubbed (preferably cultivated)

ACCOMPANIMENT

- lime wedge

DIRECTIONS

1. In a 4- to 5-quart heavy saucepan over fairly low heat, cook the onion, garlic, and ginger until the onion is tender. Stir often. Stir in the wine, juices, curry powder, thyme, saffron, bay leaf, coconut milk, tomato, and sambal oelek. After about 15 minutes of simmering with the lid ajar and stirring now and again, the liquid should be slightly reduced.
2. Sea salt should be added after cooking the cilantro and mussels covered over high heat for 3 to 4 minutes, or just long enough for the mussels to open. Serve right away.

89. DULCE DE PLÁTANO

Prep5 MIN

Total20 MIN

Ingredientes

- 4cucharadas de mantequilla
- 5plátanos maduros (plantains) cortados en pedazos o rebanadas
- 1/2taza de azúcar morena
- 2rajitas de canela en rama
- 1nuez moscada entera, si la deseas
- 5clavos de olor dulces, enteros o en polvo
- 1taza de agua

Instrucciones

1. Derrite the mantequilla in a deep cacerola or well. Place the male or female pancakes and add the sugar until they are starting to burn without allowing them to set.
2. Then add the canela, the moscada nuez, and the specialty claves.

3. Add the water toward the end, just enough to cover the surface, and allow it to evaporate until the caramel is formed.

90. DULCE DE PLÁTANO

Prep5 MIN

Total20 MIN

Ingredientes

- 4cucharadas de mantequilla
- 5plátanos maduros (plantains) cortados en pedazos o rebanadas
- 1/2taza de azúcar morena
- 2rajitas de canela en rama
- 1nuez moscada entera, si la deseas
- 5clavos de olor dulces, enteros o en polvo
- 1taza de agua

Instrucciones

1. Derrite the mantequilla in a deep cacerola or well. Place the male or female pancakes and add the sugar until they are starting to burn without allowing them to set.
2. Then add the canela, the moscada nuez, and the specialty claves.
3. Add the water toward the end, just enough to cover the surface, and allow it to evaporate until the caramel is formed.

91. GARLIC TOSTONES (FRIED GREEN PLANTAINS)

INGREDIENTS

Tostones

- 3 cups of water 750 mL
- 1 garlic clove, peel off and crushed (non-compulsory)
- 1 Tbsp salt (+ more to season) 15 mL
- 3 green plantains, peel off, slice into 1-inch thick slices
- 3 to 4 cups of canola oil (enough to fill pan about 1 inch deep) 750 mL to 1 L

Dip for Tostones

- 1/3 cup of canola oil 75 mL
- 2 Tbsp vinegar 30 mL
- 1 Tbsp lime juice 15 mL
- 1 clove garlic, chop up
- 1/4 tsp salt 1 mL
- 2 green onions, lightly chop up
- 1 Tbsp chop up cilantro 15 mL

INSTRUCTIONS

1. Mix salt, garlic, and water in a large bowl. Add the plantain slices and soak for 15 minutes. Dry thoroughly with paper towels. Put seasoned water aside. 350 °F (180 °C) is the recommended frying temperature for canola oil.
2. To begin with, fry the plantain slices for 7 to 8 minutes, or until they are crisp (do not brown). With a slotted spoon, remove and thoroughly blot with paper towels. Smash every slice of fried plantain using a tostonera (plantain press), the broad edge of a chef's knife, a tiny plate, or a small sliceting board. (At this point, tostones can be refrigerate to enjoy later when fried.) Re-dip in the salted garlic water, then take it out right away. Dry thoroughly with paper towels.

3. Reheat the oil to 375 °F (190 °C) for the second fry. Tostones should be fried for 3 to 4 minutes, rotating once, or until crisp and golden brown. Use a slotted spoon to remove. On paper towels, drain. Add salt as need and serve alongside dip.
4. Tip: Pick hard green plantains for the best results. Plantains can be peel off by trimming the ends and making three to four slashes lengthwise around the fruit. Plantain should be submerged in running water while being peel off with a paring knife.

92. SPICED GINGER SIMPLE SYRUP

Prep Time: 5 minutes

Cook Time: 30 minutes

Total Time: 35 minutes

Ingredients

- 2 ounce chunk of fresh ginger crushed or grated
- 2-3 cinnamon sticks
- 4 cloves
- 3 all spice berries
- 2 cups of sugar – could also use panela/piloncillo
- 2 cups of water use less for a thicker syrup

Instructions

1. In a small saucepan, mix all the ingredients and heat over low to medium heat.
2. Stir the sugar until all of it has dissolved.
3. Simmer for around 30 minutes on low heat.
4. After letting the syrup cool, strain it to get the ginger and spices out.
5. Use as necessary.

93. GRILLED JAMAICAN JERK PORK CHOPS

PREP TIME 30 mins

COOK TIME 14 mins

TOTAL TIME 44 mins

INGREDIENTS

- 2 bone-in pork loin chops
- 1 tablespoon allspice berries
- 1 tablespoon whole black peppercorns
- 4 to 6 whole Scotch bonnet peppers stems removed
- 6 scallions roughly chop up
- 1 large shallot peel off
- One 2 inch piece ginger peel off and roughly chop up
- 6 smashed large garlic cloves
- 3 tbsp brown sugar
- 2 tbsp fresh thyme leaves
- 2 tbsp lightly grated lime zest
- 2 tbsp fresh lime juice
- 2 tbsp canola oil
- ½ tsp freshly grated nutmeg
- 2 tsp kosher salt

INSTRUCTIONS

1. Grind the black peppercorns and allspice in a mortar and pestle.
2. Transfer the spices, together with the lime zest and juice, canola oil, nutmeg, salt, scallions, shallots, ginger, garlic, and Scotch bonnet peppers, to a food processor. until smooth, blend or process.

3. Put the pork chops in a sizable resealable bag, and using gloves, carefully pour the marinade over the chops. Then, place the bag in the refrigerator for 24 hours.
4. When it's time to cook, take the pork out of the fridge, place it on a plate, and wait an hour for it to come to room temperature before cooking.
5. Set the grill on direct grilling at 350 degrees Fahrenheit in the interim.
6. The pork chops should be grilled for 5-7 minutes on every side, or until a good char forms and the internal temperature reveryes 140°F.
7. While the carryover cooking raises the temperature to the 145°F level advised by the USDA, remove the pork chops and allow them to rest.
8. Serve alongside the mango and black bean salad.

94. GRILLED FILLET OF BEEF WITH TOMATO GINGER VINAIGRETTE

INGREDIENTS

- 2 ts Coriander seeds; crushed
- 2 tb Fresh Lemon Juice
- 1 1/2 lb Fillet of beef; trimmed and
- 2 ts Soy sauce
- 1 tb Lightly grated peel off fresh
- 1 ts Dijon mustard
- 1/3 c olive oil
- 3 Garlic cloves; chop up fine
- 1/2 ts Dried hot red pepper flakes

INSTRUCTIONS

1. Making a marinade Incorporate the marinade ingredients, add salt and pepper as need, and a big jar with a tight-fitting lid. Shake vigorously to mix. Mix the fillet and marinade in a sizable plastic bag that can be sealed, pressing out as much air as you can. Put the fillet in a shallow dish or bowl after turning the bag several times to coat it with marinade. Fillet should be marinated for at least 8 hours or overnight, rotating the bag every few hours. Before grilling, let the fillet rest at room temperature for 30 minutes. grill or grill pan preparation. The fillet should be

cooked until a meat thermometer reads 130 to 135 degrees, or about 25 to 30 minutes for medium-rare, on an oiled rack placed 5 to 6 inches over hot coals. Turn the fillet every 5 minutes to ensure that both sides are uniformly seared. (Alternatively, a fillet may be grilled on a grill pan for about the same amount of time, or it may be roasted on an oiled roasting pan in a preheated 500 degree oven.) After moving the fillet to a chopping board, give it 10 minutes to stand. 2 servings + leftovers from the yield. Cooking Live Show #CL8937 submitted the recipe. On September 15, 1997, "Angele and Jon Freeman" posted a recipe to MC-Recipe Digest V1 #781.

95. GRILLED PINEAPPLE WITH VANILLA MASCARPONE

Prep25 mins

Cook15 mins

Total40 mins

INGREDIENTS

- 1 cup of dark rum
- 1 1/2 sticks (6 oz) unsalted butter
- 1/4 cup of light brown sugar
- 1 vanilla bean
- 8 ounces mascarpone*
- 1 ripe pineapple peel off and split into 1/4-inch-thick rounds
- 1/2 cup of fresh blueberries

DIRECTIONS

2. In a small saucepan, mix the rum, butter, and sugar. Simmer, whisking often, for about 10 minutes, or until the sugar has melted and the mixture has slightly thickened. (The glaze can be prepared a few days beforehand, cooled, covered, and stored in the fridge. Before usage, bring to room temperature.)
3. With the tip of a sharp knife, split the vanilla bean in half lengthwise, then scrape out the seeds. Mascarpone and vanilla bean seeds are mixd in a whisk. Mascarpone can be prepared a day ahead of time, covered, and kept chilled.
4. Your grill should be quite hot.
5. Grill the pineapple slices for 2 to 3 minutes on every side, coating regularly with the glaze until golden.
6. Remove the pineapple and transfer it to a dish or serving plates. Place a dollop of vanilla mascarpone on top of every piece. Add a few fresh blueberries as a garnish. Serve right away.

96. GUAVA-STUFFED CHICKEN WITH CARAMELIZED MANGO

Ready In: 1hr

INGREDIENTS

- 3/4cup of olive oil
- 1/4cup of fresh lemon juice
- 6garlic cloves, chop up
- 3tbsp chop up fresh parsley
- 2tbsp fresh thyme leaves
- 6large chicken breasts (skinless & boneless)
- 3ounces cream cheese, room temperature
- 2tbsp guava paste (about 1 1/2 oz)
- 2 1/2ounces fresh spinach leaves, chop up (2 cups of loosely packed)
- 2tbsp canola oil
- 1/2cup of dry whte wine
- 1/2cup of low sodium chicken broth

- 4tbsp butter (1/2 stick)
- 1large mango, halved, pitted, peel off, slice into 1/2 inch slices

DIRECTIONS

1. In a big bowl, mix the first five ingredients; add the chicken breasts and toss to coat.
2. Chill the chicken breasts for 3 to 4 hours while turning them occasionally.
3. In a medium bowl, mix the cream cheese and guava paste by whisking.
4. Stir in the spinach; cover and chill for at least two hours until somewhat hard; transfer to a pastry bag or a zip-lock bag with the corner slice off.
5. Take out 1 chicken breast from the marinade, reserving the remaining marinade in the bowl.
6. Insert a small, sharp knife into the chicken breast's one side, moving it in an arc to create a huge pocket while maintaining a 1 1/4-inch aperture.
7. the remaining chicken, and repeat.
8. Chicken breasts' apertures can be filled by piping filling into the pockets.
9. Use toothpicks or metal turkey pins to close any gaps.
10. Two heavy, large skillets, every with a tablespoon of canola oil, are heated over medium heat.
11. Every skillet should include 3 chicken breasts. Cook every side for 3 minutes or until browned.
12. Add wine and broth to the second pan along with any liquids from the first skillet, and then bring the second skillet to a boil.
13. To the wine mixture in the skillet, add the chicken breasts.
14. Cover the skillet, lower the heat to medium, and simmer the chicken for about 10 minutes, basting as needed.
15. Move the chicken to a work surface and give it 10 minutes to stand.
16. Melt butter in a different heavy big skillet over medium-high heat in the meantime.
17. Add the mango slices and cook for two minutes on every side, or until golden.
18. Chicken should be slice into 1/2 inch-thick slices.
19. Place the chicken on the platter.
20. Boil fluids in a skillet for 3 minutes, or until they've slightly thickened and the sauce has been reduced to 3/4 cup of.
21. Place mango around the chicken and drizzle sauce over it.

97. VEGAN HAITIAN SOUP JOUMOU

PREP TIME 30 mins

COOK TIME 2 hrs 30 mins

TOTAL TIME 3 hrs

INGREDIENTS

- 2 Pumpkins 7lbs. Total. One pumpkin 4 Lbs and the other 3 Lbs. Best to use Calabaza squash or butternut squash
- 3 Cups of Elbow Macaroni – We used organic elbow macaroni. Feel free to substitute with a gluten free version if needed.
- 1 Tbsp. Fresh Ginger Grated
- 8 Large Carrots Slice into about 8 pieces every
- 1 Cabbage; About 2lbs.
- 6 Tsp. Salt Or As need
- 3 Tsp. Ground Black Pepper Or As need
- 6 Cloves Or 2 Tsp. Ground Cloves
- 5 Garlic Cloves
- Juice From 3 Lemons
- Herbs; About 5 Sage Leaves 7 sprigs Fresh Parsley, & About 8 Sprigs Of Fresh Thyme
- 6 Tbsp. Better Than Bouillon Paste Vegetable Base
- 4 Tbsp. Olive Oil
- 32 Oz. Vegetable Broth
- 12 Cups of Water; Separated – 10 Cups of Water To Cook The Pumpkin And 2 Cups of To Add To The Soup
- 5 Green Onions; Chop up

- 1 Lb. Gold Potatoes; Slice Into Quarters
- 1 Large Onion; Roughly Chop up

INSTRUCTIONS

1. Prepare your ingredients first: Olive oil, Better than Bouillon Paste, Herbs, Lemon Juice, Salt, Pepper, Cloves, Ginger, and Macaroni should be set aside.
2. the pumpkin in great detail. Take out all the dirt and trash. Pumpkin should be slice into small chunks. If you do not have a good blender, peel the pumpkin. We didn't peel the pumpkin, though. Throw away the seeds and internal flesh.
3. The pumpkin and 10 cups of water should be put in a sizable 12-quart stockpot. Bring to a boil and then simmer until fork-tender.
4. Prepare the other ingredients while the pumpkin is cooking.
5. Carrots should be peel off, chop up into 6 to 8 pieces, washed, and placed away.
6. The potatoes should then be peel off, quartered, washed, and left aside in water.
7. Then, slice or chop the cabbage into small or medium-sized pieces. In water, wash and set aside. Avoid slicing the cabbage too thinly since when mixd with the other ingredients, it may overcook.
8. Wash and chop the onions before putting them aside. After washing and chopping the green onions and garlic, leave aside.
9. Remove the stockpot from the heat once the pumpkin has finished cooking, leaving the cooked pumpkin in the water.
10. When the oil is hot enough, add the onions, green onions, ginger, and garlic to a large skillet over medium-high heat. Cook until translucency and caramelization are achieved. Cooking finished, put the skillet away.
11. Return the stockpot to the burner, then puree the squash with an immersion blender over medium heat. Transfer the squash and liquid to a top-notch blender if you don't have an immersion blender. Return to the stockpot once blended.
12. The sautéed garlic, onions, and green peppers should then be added to the pureed pumpkin.
13. Potatoes, cabbage, carrots, herbs, 2 cups of water, vegetable broth—better than bouillon paste, salt, pepper, crushed cloves, and lemon juice—come next. Bring to a boil over high heat, then turn down to medium after it begins to boil.
14. Add the pasta when the cabbage is almost done cooking. Over medium-low heat, bring to a simmer for around 15 to 20 minutes. Occasionally stir the mixture to prevent the bottom from sticking.
15. As the soup joumou simmers, it will thicken. Serve in a bowl along with French bread.

NOTES

1. The soup will continue to thicken as it sets; when you're ready to eat, thin it out with water if required.
2. To prevent the cloves from floating in the soup while adding them, place them inside a piece of onion. It will be simpler to take out once the soup has finished cooking.
3. Please deselect the camera when printing the recipe so that the images are NOT printed with the recipe (if preferred).
4. Calories per serving are approximations.
5. Please note that this article may contain affiliate links. See our complete Privacy Statement. By selecting the links and/or completing a purchase, we might be paid.

NUTRITION

Serving: 12PeopleCalories: 831kcalCarbs: 104gProtein: 43gFat: 27gSat fat: 2gPolyunSat fat: 1gMonounSat fat: 4gCholesterol: 87mgSodium: 1836mgPotassium: 1241mgFiber: 13gSugar: 13gVit. A: 15IUVit. C: 59mgCalcium: 12mgIron: 29mg

98. PICKLED CABBAGE RECIPE

PREP TIME5 mins

COOK TIME5 mins

TOTAL TIME10 mins

INGREDIENTS

- 1 bag Tri-color coleslaw mix 1 lb.
- 6 Habanero Peppers or Scotch Bonnet Peppers. Chop up. Wear gloves when handling hot peppers
- Juice From 1 Lemon
- 2 Tsp. Kosher Salt
- 2 Cups of Distilled White Vinegar

- 2 Tsp. Lemon Pepper Seasoning

INSTRUCTIONS

1. Put every ingredient in a large basin. Assemble by thoroughly combining.
2. Before serving, place in an airtight container and chill for up to two hours.

NOTES

- Both the text and the images have been updated.
- Because the chili peppers are so hot and spicy, it is strongly advised that you handle them while wearing gloves to prevent scorching to your hands (and face or eyes if touched thereafter).
- Although it is uncommon in Haitian pikliz, lemon pepper is used in this recipe because it improves the flavor of this side dish.
- The cabbage and carrots may soften slightly but keep their crunch after a few days, adding texture to any dish.
- This cheerful pikliz is wonderful for family gatherings, bevery parties, and backyard get-togethers at any time of the year.
- In an airtight container, pikliz often keep for up to 6 months in the refrigerator. As the liquid level drops, merely add vinegar.
- It's also an excellent idea to store pikliz in a mason jar.
- Calories per serving are approximations.

NUTRITION

Serving: 36PeopleCalories: 215kcalCarbs: 46gProtein: 7gSodium: 2999mgPotassium: 1230 mgFiber: 14gSugar: 28gVit. A: 7950IUVit. C: 503.3mgCalcium: 230mgIron: 2.5mg

99. HANGER STEAKS WITH 125TH STREET MALANGA MASH

PREP TIME

20 minutes

TOTAL TIME

Ingredients

- 4 hanger steaks weighing 10 to 12 ounces, trimmed of fat, sinew, and central connective tissue
- tsp of adobo seasoning powder
- fresh orange juice, 1/2 cup of
- fresh lemon juice, 1/4 cup of
- White wine vinegar, 2 tsp
- Canola oil, separated into 4 tbsp, for the 125th Street Malanga Mash (click for recipe)

Preparation

1. Add adobo seasoning to steaks. Place in a 13x9x2 inch glass baking dish in a single layer. Pour vinegar, orange juice, and lemon juice into a bowl and add the steaks. For one hour, marinate at room temperature.
2. In every of two heavy, large skillets, heat 2 tbsp of oil over medium-high heat. Steaks should be taken out of the marinade and seasoned. 2 steaks should be added to

every skillet, and they should be cooked for 6 minutes per side for medium-rare. Serve with mashed malanga.
3. Your recipes from Epicurious and Bon Appétit have come to an end. Now subscribe. Sign In if you're already a subscriber.

100. ISLAND PORK TENDERLOIN (NON-COMPULSORY SALAD)

Ready In: 1hr 30mins

INGREDIENTS

FOR PORK

- 2tsp salt
- 1/2tsp black pepper
- 1tsp ground cumin
- 1tsp chili powder
- 1tsp cinnamon
- 2(1 lb) pork tenderloin (approx. weight)
- 2tbsp olive oil

FOR GLAZE

- 1cup of dark brown sugar (not light)
- 2tbsp lightly chop up garlic
- 1tablespoon hot sauce (Tabasco)

FOR SALAD VINAIGRETTE

- 3tbsp fresh lime juice
- 1tablespoon fresh orange juice
- 1tablespoon Dijon mustard
- 1tsp curry powder

- 1/2tsp salt
- 1/4tsp black pepper
- 1/2cup of olive oil

FOR SALAD

- 3navel oranges
- 5ounces baby spinach leaves, trimmed (6 cups of)
- 4cups of napa cabbage, thinly split (from 1 medium head)
- 1red bell pepper, slice lengthwise into thin strips
- 1/2cup of golden raisin
- 2avocados

DIRECTIONS

1. Oven: Preheat to 350 degrees.
2. Rub spices over meat after combining salt, pepper, cumin, chili powder, and cinnamon.
3. Pork should be browned, flipping once, for a total of four minutes, in an ovenproof 12-inch heavy skillet with moderately high heat until just starting to smoke. Pork remains in skillet.
4. Brown sugar, garlic, and Tabasco are mixd to make a glaze, which is then applied to every tenderloin before roasting the meat. Roast in the middle of the oven for about 20 minutes, or until a thermometer inserted diagonally in the center of every tenderloin reads 140°F. Give the pork 10 minutes to warm up in the skillet. (While standing, the temperature will increase to roughly 155°F.)
5. Make vinaigrette while roasting the pork:
6. Blend the juices with the mustard, curry powder, salt, and pepper. Add the oil in a stream while whisking to create an emulsion.
7. AS THE PORK STANDS, PREPARE THE SALAD INGREDIENTS:
8. With a sharp knife, remove orange peel, including the white pith, before slicing every orange crosswise into slices that are 1/4 inch thick. In a big bowl, mix spinach, cabbage, bell pepper, raisins, and about 1/4 cup of vinaigrette. Avocados should be peel off, pitted, and halved before being slice into 1/4-inch-thick slices.
9. MIX SALAD:
10. Slice the pork into 1/2-inch-thick slices at a 45-degree angle. Split pork, oranges, and avocados should be arranged in rows on top of a huge tray of dressed salad.

Pour some vinaigrette over the oranges and avocados. Pork should be covered with any skillet juices.

101. JAMAICAN HOT PEPPER SHRIMP

Prep Time: 2 minutes

Cook Time: 1 hour 13 minutes

Total Time: 1 hour 15 minutes

Ingredients

- 1 lb of raw shrimp with shell
- 3 red scotch bonnet lightly chop up
- ½ tablespoon of onion powder
- ½ tablespoon of garlic granules or powder
- 1-2 tsp of himalayan pink salt
- ½ tsp of black pepper
- 1 tablespoon of sweet paprika
- 3 garlic cloves chop up
- ¼ tsp of allspice
- ½ tablespoon of thyme non-compulsory
- fresh lime to clean the shrimp
- 1 tsp of old bay seasoning non-compulsory
- ¼ cup of warm water
- ½ tsp annatto powder non-compulsory, for a deeper, natural hue of red

Instructions

1. After rubbing the shrimp with lime juice, thoroughly rinse them with water.
2. With the use of a toothpick, remove the shrimp's intestinal tract and throw it away. Remove the legs and antennae as well (if desired).
3. Rub all of the ingredients into the shrimp and let them sit for an hour to infuse.
4. Use 1-2 tbsp of coconut oil to preheat the dutch oven on medium heat.
5. Lower the shrimp into the pot with a slotted spoon and stir for two minutes.
6. If using, add the annatto powder and 1/4 cup of heated water. Cover the lid, and let the mixture gently steam for 10 minutes. The shrimp should be pink and ready to eat; as it cools, the sauce will thicken.
7. Once prepared, serve right away to avoid the shrimp's texture changing due to reheating.

Notes

- Use my Seafood Seasoning if you want to change the seasoning.
- Simply add additional paprika, food coloring, or annatto—about a half tsp should do—to give your shrimp a reddish hue.
- Use this link as a reference if you've never cleaned shrimp before.
- You're welcome to offer the shrimp in a tiny clear plastic bag like the street vendors do.
- Old bay seasoning is non-compulsory and not included in the original recipe; this is my own adaptation.
- If you want it to be hotter, add additional scotch bonnet.
- If you can't get scotch bonnets, substitute chilli, habanero, or scorpion peppers.
- It is strongly advised to utilize raw shrimp with heads and tails rather than cooked ones.
- When cooking, keep an eye on the shrimp; once they turn pink, they are prepared; the cooking time is an estimate.

Nutrition

Calories: 138kcal | Carbs: 6g | Protein: 24g | Fat: 2g | Sat fat: 1g | Cholesterol: 286mg | Sodium: 1467mg | Potassium: 193mg | Fiber: 2g | Sugar: 1g | Vit. A: 975IU | Vit. C: 22mg | Calcium: 185mg | Iron: 3mg

102. JAMAICAN JERK CHICKEN

Active Time: 30 mins

Total Time: 9 hrs

Yield: 8

Ingredients

- 1 medium onion, coarsely chop up
- 3 medium scallions, chop up
- 2 Scotch bonnet chiles, chop up
- 2 garlic cloves, chop up
- 1 tablespoon five-spice powder
- 1 tablespoon allspice berries, coarsely ground
- 1 tablespoon coarsely ground pepper
- 1 tsp dried thyme, crumbled
- 1 tsp freshly grated nutmeg
- 1 tsp salt
- 1/2 cup of soy sauce
- 1 tablespoon vegetable oil
- Two 3 1/2- to 4-pound chickens, quartered

Directions

1. The onion, scallions, chiles, garlic, five-spice powder, allspice, pepper, thyme, nutmeg, and salt should be mixd in a food processor and processed to a coarse paste. Add the soy sauce and oil slowly while the machine is running. In a big, shallow dish, pour the marinade, add the chicken, and toss to coat. Overnight, cover and chill. Before continuing, let the chicken come to room temperature.
2. Start the grill. For 35 to 40 minutes, grill the chicken over a medium-hot flame, turning it over once or twice, until it is thoroughly browned and cooked. (Cover the grill to add more smokiness.) Serve the chicken after transferring it to a plate.

103. JAMAICAN JERK POTATO SALAD

Ingredients

- 450g red potatoes, chop up (skin on)
- 4 tbsp Country Range Light Mayonnaise
- 1 tbsp Country Range Jamaican Jerk Seasoning
- 6 spring onions, split

Method

1. The potatoes should only be barely cooked after 10 to 15 minutes of boiling.
2. Mix the Jamaican Jerk seasoning with the mayonnaise.
3. In a serving bowl, mix the potatoes, mayonnaise, and spring onions.
4. At room temperature, serve.
5. 15 to 20 minutes
6. Main

104. JAMAICAN JERK MARINADE RECIPE

Prep Time: 10 minutes

Cook Time: 1 minute

Total Time: 11 minutes

Ingredients

- 4-6 Scotch Bonnet peppers chop up
- 1 small red onion chop up
- 4-6 garlic cloves chop up
- 4 stalks scallions end trimmed
- 1/4 cup of soy sauce
- 1/4 cup of vinegar (use white vinegar or apple cider vinegar to your preference)
- 2 tbsp olive oil
- Juice from 1 large orange about ¾ cup of (orange juice)
- Juice from half a lime lime juice
- 1 tablespoon freshly grated ginger
- 2 tbsp brown sugar
- 1 tsp nutmeg
- 1 tsp allspice
- 1 tsp cinnamon
- 1 tsp dried thyme or use fresh if available
- Salt and pepper as need I usually use 1 tsp salt and 1 tablespoon black pepper

Instructions

1. All the ingredients should be placed in a food processor. until smooth, process.
2. To marinate your chicken, pork, fish, or veggies, use right away.

Notes

- a medium-hot level of heat. Scotch Bonnets, which are quite similar to habanero peppers in both heat and flavor, will give you a good amount of heat. More Scotch Bonnet peppers, spicier peppers, or chili flakes can be used to amp up the intensity. Reduce the amount of Scotch Bonnets or swap them out with milder peppers to lessen the intensity.

utrition Information

Calories: 63kcal   Carbs: 6g   Protein: 1g   Fat: 3g   Sodium: 408mg   Potassium: 74mg   Sugar : 4g   Vit. A: 105IU   Vit. C: 9.8mg   Calcium: 21mg   Iron: 0.5mg

105. JERK PORK RECIPE

Prep Time15 mins

Cook Time6 hrs

Total Time6 hrs 15 mins

Ingredients

- 3 Pound Boneless Pork Butt – trimmed of fat & slice into 2-inch chunks
- 2 TBS Neutral Oil – such as canola or vegetable (SEE NOTES)
- 4 TBS Jerk Seasoning – homemade or store-bought (SEE NOTES)
- Kosher Salt - as need
- 1 Bunch Green Onion – slice into 3-inch pieces
- 3 Cloves Garlic – smashed & peel off
- 1-2 Jalapeno or Habanero Peppers – stemmed & roughly chop up (SEE NOTES)
- ½-inch Piece Fresh Ginger – peel off and split
- ¾ Cup of Fresh Orange Juice - (from about 4 oranges)
- ¼ Cup of Fresh Lime Juice – (from about 2 limes)
- 1 TBS EVERY: Dark Brown Sugar and Low Sodium-Soy Sauce

- Pineapple Salsa: (yield about 2 cups of)
- 1 ½ Cups of Fresh Diced Pineapple
- 1 Jalapeno – stemmed, seeded & lightly diced
- ¼ Red Onion – lightly diced
- 2-3 TBS Cilantro Leaves – chop up
- 2-3 TBS Fresh Lime Juice
- 1 tsp Honey
- For Garnish: Split Scallions, Microgreens, Fresh Thyme
- For Serving: Lime Wedges, Slices of Avocado, Rice or Slaw

Instructions

1. Pork should be seasoned after being patted dry with paper towels on a clean work surface. Place the pork in a big bowl and top with oil (SEE NOTES). Coat by tossing. Sprinkle some jerk seasoning over the pork. As need, add salt to the dish. The pork should be well coated after being mixed and tossed with tongs or your hands. (NOTE: Because the mixture will be spicy, you might wish to wear gloves. After washing your hands, avoid touching your face or eyes!
2. To marinate, wrap the bowl in plastic wrap or transfer it to a sizable zip-top bag, then chill for at least three hours or better yet, overnight.
3. Mix into the slow cooker: While you prepare the other ingredients, take the pork out of the refrigerator and let it sit at room temperature for 30 minutes. Put the pork in the slow cooker's 5–6 quart bowl. Add the ginger, orange and lime juices, sugar, soy sauce, onions, garlic, and peppers.
4. Cook: Place the pork in the slow cooker with the lid on and cook for 6-7 hours on LOW, or until the meat readily shreds with a fork.
5. Make the salsa while the pork is cooking: In a medium bowl, mix all the salsa's components. Salt is used to flavor. Taste, then season as needed. Keep chilled until you're ready to use.
6. Delete fat and strain liquid: Remove and discard the fat from the top of the slow cooker's cooking liquid. Pour the cooking liquid through a strainer into a basin or measuring cup of.
7. FOR CRISP PORK ONLY: Pork should be moved with a slotted spoon to a big, foil-covered sheet pan with a rim. Place oven rack in upper-middle portion of oven. Set the oven to BRILLIANT.
8. Non-compulsory - Broil: Gently mix the pork with 14 to 12 cup of the drained cooking liquid. For 3 to 5 minutes, or until crisp, broil. Take the pork out of the oven, turn it over, and add an additional 1/4 to 1/2 cup of cooking liquid. extra 3–5 minutes of broiling NOTE: Pork can move from golden brown and crispy to burnt very rapidly in the oven.

9. To serve, place the pork in a serving bowl and top with some of the cooking liquid. Serve hot with salsa over rice or in your favorite tacos! Enjoy!

Notes

- You can use premade seasoning, however I prefer to create my own. If using store-bought, we suggest Walkerswood or Grace wet jerk seasoning, both of which have the consistency of paste. Leave off the neutral oil if you're using jerk flavor paste or marinade. Click HERE for the homemade jerk seasoning recipe.
- Use one jalapeño pepper if you don't like a lot of spice. Before following the recipe's instructions, make sure to remove the pepper's seeds and ribs. Use two jalapenos and leave the seeds in the pepper if you prefer mild heat. Try using a habanero pepper if you prefer medium heat; you can either leave the seeds in for a milder to medium heat or eliminate them for a hotter medium heat. Use two habanero peppers if you prefer your food spicy.
- The nutritional data is an estimate based on 6 servings and excludes salsa.

Nutrition

Calories: 384kcal | Carbs: 10g | Protein: 44g | Fat: 18g | Sat fat: 5g | Cholesterol: 136mg | Sodium: 237mg | Potassium: 964mg | Fiber: 2g | Sugar: 5g | Vit. A: 1708IU | Vit. C: 23mg | Calcium: 58mg | Iron: 4mg

106. KEY LIME CHEESECAKE WITH MANGO RIBBONS

Makes 8 to 10 servings

Total Time under 4 hours

Ingredients

- 1 1/4 cups of fine graham cracker crumbs (5 oz)
- 3 tbsp sugar

- 1/2 stick (1/4 cup of) unsalted butter, melted
- 2 (8-oz) packages cream cheese at room temperature
- 1 cup of + 2 tbsp sugar
- 3/4 cup of fresh Key lime juice (strained from about 1 1/2 lb Key limes) or bottled
- 1/2 cup of sour cream
- 1/2 tsp vanilla
- 2 1/2 tbsp all-purpose flour
- 1/4 tsp salt
- 3 large eggs
- 2 large firm-ripe mangoes
- 1 tablespoon fresh Key lime juice (strained) or bottled
- 1/2 cup of chilled heavy cream
- 1 tablespoon sugar

Instructions

1. To make the crust, grease the bottom and sides of a springform pan and preheat the oven to 350°F.
2. Crumb mixture, sugar, and butter are thoroughly mixed in a bowl with a fork. After that, press mixture uniformly into bottom and up one-third of pan's side. Crust should bake for 8 minutes in the center of the oven before cooling on a rack.
3. Produce filling:
4. Lower the oven's setting to 325°F.
5. Using an electric mixer, whip cream cheese at medium speed until frothy before adding sugar. Blend in the lime juice, sour cream, and vanilla after adding them. When the flour and salt are barely mixd, add the eggs all at once and mix just until they are mixd on low speed, scraping down the side as necessary.
6. After adding the filling, place the springform plate in a shallow baking dish. Bake cake in center of oven for 1 to 1 hour and 10 minutes, or until center is set. On a rack, let the springform pan cool fully. (The cake will keep setting as it cools.)
7. Remove the side of the pan by running a thin knife around the cake's edge. If preferred, move cake to a serving platter using a sizable metal spatula.
8. Produce topping:

9. Mandoline slices mangoes very thinly (less than 1/8 inch thick), keeping the fruit whole. Caution is advised because peel off mango is slick. Slice long, hefty slices in half. Mango slices and lime juice should be gently mixed.
10. Spread over cheesecake after whipping cream and sugar in a bowl with an electric mixer until just holding stiff peaks. Mango slices should be bent and curled before being arranged artistically over cream.

107. KEY LIME MASCARPONE "CANNOLI" WITH MANGO SAUCE

INGREDIENTS

- 5 tb Unsalted butter ; slice into bits, softened
- Mango Sauce

FOR "CANNOLI" SHELLS

- 3/4 c Sweetened flaked coconut
- parchment paper
- 2 tb All-purpose flour
- 4 4" long cannoli forms ; 5/8-inch in diameter
- 4 tb Key lime juice
- 1/2 c Granulated sugar
- 2 Firmly packed tb light brown sugar

FOR FILLING

ACCOMPANIMENTS

- 1/3 c Granulated sugar
- 4 oz Cream cheese ; softened
- 2 ts lime zest ; Freshly grated
- carambola ; Split
- 1 tb milk
- 1 c Mascarpone cheese
- Fresh raspberries

INSTRUCTIONS

1. Construct "cannoli" shells: Lightly grease a large baking sheet and preheat the oven to 350 degrees. On a baking sheet, arrange 4 parchment squares. (Butter or oil helps parchment squares adhere to the baking sheet.) Coconut and flour should be processed in a food processor until the coconut is lightly ground. Blend in the milk, sugars, and butter until the dough comes together in a ball, about 10 seconds. Every of the 4 parchment squares should have a well-rounded tsp of dough on it. Spread the dough out evenly into 2 inch rounds using slightly damp fingertips. Bake cookies in the center of the oven for 10 minutes, or until they are very thin and golden brown. Immediately move the cookies (still on the parchment) to a rack and let them stand there for 30 to 45 seconds, or until they are just stiff enough to keep their shape. Roll a cookie swiftly around a cannoli form to form a cylinder, working with 1 cookie at a time and using parchment as a helper. (If cookies get too hard to roll, put them back in the oven for a minute on a baking sheet with paper.) Before removing the cannoli form, cool the formed biscuits or the rack. Make additional cookies using the leftover dough in the same way, baking and shaping them in groups of four while letting the baking sheet cool completely in between. The cookie is delicate. Cookies last four days when kept in a single layer in an airtight container. Produce filling: Mascarpone should be added after smoothing out the cream cheese, sugar, lime juice, and zest in a bowl with an electric mixer. Covered, chill the filling for at least 4 hours and up to a day until it is firm. Create the dessert: Filling should be whisked before being placed in a pastry bag with a 1/4-inch plain or fancy tip. 12 cookies should have filled carefully piped into both ends. Six dessert plates should every have about 1/4 cup of mango sauce. Distribute the sauce equally by tilting the plate. Add two "cannoli," raspberries, and slices of carambola on top. 6 portions;

Gourmet May 1995 2231 calories (kcal), 150g total fat (59 percent of calories from fat), 17g protein, 214g Carb, 438mg cholesterol, and 431mg sodium are contained in one serving. Exchanges: 0 Fruit, 0 Vegetable, 0 Grain(Starch), 2 Lean Meat, 29 Fat, and 13 Other Carbs. by MM Buster v2.0n, who converted.

108. LAMB CHOPS WITH MASHED SWEET POTATOES AND ONIONS

Ingredients

Sauce

- 2 tbsp olive oil
- 4 pounds meaty lamb neck bones, slice into 2-inch pieces
- 2 onions, split
- 4 cups of canned low-salt chicken broth
- 2 cups of canned beef broth
- 8 large garlic cloves, halved
- 6 fresh thyme sprigs

Sweet Potatoes

- 2 large tan-skinned sweet potatoes (about 1 3/4 pounds), peel off, slice into 1/2-inch-thick rounds
- 3 tbsp butter
- 1 onion, split
- 2 tsp chop up fresh thyme
- Pinch of ground cloves
- 8 3- to 4-ounce lamb chops (about 1 inch thick)
- 2 tbsp (about) olive oil

INSTRUCTIONS

2. In a heavy, big Dutch oven, heat the oil over high heat. Working in batches, add the lamb bones; sauté for about 10 minutes, stirring frequently, until well-browned. Place the bones on a plate. Add the onion and cook for 12 minutes or until it turns brown. Dutch oven with the bones back. Bring to a boil the two broths, the garlic, and the thyme. Reduce heat, cover slightly, and simmer Dutch oven for two hours.
3. Press firmly on particles to force liquid out of sauce as you strain it into a sturdy small saucepan. Throw away solids. Boil sauce for 20 minutes or until it has reduced to 2/3 cup of. Offload fat by spooning it. Discard the sauce.
4. Regarding sweet potatoes:
5. Sweet potatoes should be cooked for around 13 minutes in a big saucepan of salted boiling water. Drain. In a large, heavy skillet set over medium-high heat, melt the butter. Add the onion and lightly chop up thyme, and cook for 10 minutes, or until the onion is golden brown. Mixture of sweet potatoes and onions should be transferred to a processor and almost completely pureed. Add cloves and stir. Add salt and pepper as need. (Sweet potatoes and sauce can be made a day in advance. Separately wrap and chill.)
6. Salt and pepper the lamb before serving. In a big skillet, heat 1 tablespoon of oil over high heat. Add the lamb in batches and cook it for 4 minutes per side for medium-rare, adding additional oil to the skillet as needed.
7. Sauce should be simmering in the interim. In a medium skillet over low heat, rewarm sweet potatoes by tossing frequently.
8. On every of the four dishes, place a generous spoonful of potatoes in the middle. Add 2 chops to every. Pour sauce on top. Put some thyme sprigs on top.

109. MANGO LIME SYRUP

Ready In: 45mins

INGREDIENTS

- 4cups of ripe mangoes, chop up (about 2 one pound mangoes)
- 3/4cup of sugar
- 1/2cup of water
- 2tbsp fresh lime juice (as need)

DIRECTIONS

1. Mangoes should be processed until very lightly chop up.
2. Mangoes, sugar, and water are brought to a boil in a heavy medium saucepan while being constantly stirred to dissolve the sugar. Reduce heat, cover, and simmer for about 30 minutes, stirring occasionally, until mangoes are extremely soft. Stir in the lime juice and strain the mixture through a fine-mesh sieve into a basin, gently pressing on the particles as you go. Covered, cool, then chill.

110. MANGOES FLAMBÉ

Ingredients

- 4 (1-pound) firm-ripe mangoes
- 6 tbsp turbinado sugar such as Sugar in the Raw
- 1/3 cup of dark rum

INSTRUCTIONS

1. Heat the broiler.
2. Mangos are washed and dried. With a sharp knife, remove the two flat sides of every mango, sliceting lengthwise beside the pit and as close to the pit as you can, dividing the mango flesh into two substantial pieces (reserve remaining fruit for another use). Using a tiny, sharp knife, slice across the fruit at intervals of 1/2 inch, stopping short of piercing through, creating a crosshatch pattern. To make the flesh side convex, grasp the fruit at both ends and turn it inside out.
3. Place fruit in a large shallow baking pan covered with foil, skin side down. Sprinkle 4 tbsp of turbinado sugar over the fruit in a uniform layer (total). Fruit should be broiled for about 5 minutes, 5 inches from the heat, until golden brown (it will not brown evenly). On a big dish, arrange the fruit.
4. In a small saucepan over fairly low heat, mix the rum and remaining sugar until the sugar is dissolved. Remove from heat, gently light rum with a kitchen match, and then drizzle over warm mangoes while it is still blazing. Serve right away.

111. SOFRITO GRILLED BREAD

Ingredients

- 1 cup of chop up red bell pepper (about 1 small)
- 1/2 cup of chop up onion (about 1 small)
- 1/4 cup of packed fresh coriander sprigs, washed well and spun dry
- 2 garlic cloves, chop up
- 1 tsp dried oregano, crumbled
- 1/2 tsp cumin seeds
- twelve 1/4-inch-thick slices nonfat country-style bread (12 ounces total)

INSTRUCTIONS

1. All components (apart from the bread) should be blended until smooth. Sofrito should be simmered for three minutes while stirring, then seasoned with salt and pepper. A chilled, covered sofrito can be prepared two days in advance.
2. ready the grill.
3. Slice bread slices in half, if desired. Spread some sofrito on one side of every slice of bread (reserving any leftover sofrito for another use) and grill for about two minutes, sofrito side down, on an oiled rack placed 5 to 6 inches over hot coals. (Alternatively, bread can be grilled over fairly high heat in a hot, well-seasoned, ridged grill pan.) With tongs, transfer the grilled sofrito bread to a bread basket.

Nutrition Per Serving

Every serving about 124.5 calories and 0.7 grams fat (5% of calories from fat)

Made in United States
Orlando, FL
10 May 2024